WE HAD A DREAM

Eyewitnesses to the struggle for justice and equality

WE HAD A DREAM

Eyewitnesses to the struggle for justice and equality

Bernard Marin

Published in Australia by Sid Harta Books & Print Pty Ltd,
ABN: 34632585293
23 Stirling Crescent, Glen Waverley, Victoria 3150 Australia
Telephone: +61 3 9560 9920, Facsimile: +61 3 9545 1742
E-mail: author@sidharta.com.au

First published in Australia 2022
This edition published 2023
Copyright © Bernard Marin 2022
Cover design, typesetting: WorkingType (www.workingtype.com.au)

The right of Bernard Marin to be identified as the Author of the Work
has been asserted in accordance with the Copyright, Designs and Patents Act 1988.

Every effort has been made to identify copyright holders and obtain their permission for the use of copyright material. Please notify the author of any additions or corrections at bernardm@marinaccountants.com.au

All rights reserved. No part of this publication may be reproduced,
stored in a retrieval system, or transmitted, in any form or by any means without the prior written permission of the publisher, nor be otherwise circulated in any form of binding or cover other than that in which it is published and without a similar condition being imposed on the subsequent purchaser.

Bernard Marin AM
We Had a Dream
ISBN: 978-1-922958-03-7 (paperback)
978-0-6456941-9-2 (ebook)

ABOUT THE AUTHOR

Bernard Marin AM was born in 1950 and graduated from the Prahran College of Advanced Education in Melbourne in 1970. He established his accounting practice in 1981 and currently works with the staff and partners of the practice as a consultant. Bernard has held a number of positions on various boards, including: Treasurer – Melbourne Writers Festival (2005–16), Koorie Heritage Trust (2000–12) and Liberty Victoria (1984–92); board member – Australian Centre for Jewish Civilisation (2009–15), Reichstein Foundation (2011–12) and Melbourne Community Foundation (2009–10). From 1984 to 1992 Bernard was treasurer at Liberty Victoria.

Bernard lives in Melbourne with his wife Wendy.

By the same author

My Father, My Father
Good as Gold
Stories of Profit and Loss
Stories of Remembering and Forgetting
Letter to my Father
People Who Have Changed the World: Imagined interviews

Coming Soon

Breakfast with Paul: We beg to differ
Surviving: My story

These titles can be found at bernardmarin.com.au

AUTHOR'S NOTE

While I have endeavoured to be rigorous in my research, I make no claim as to the factual accuracy of my portrayal of the historical figures mentioned in each story. The actual encounters and conversations that appear in this book are works of my imagination. Like all historical fiction, the narratives in this book draw inspiration from the lives of the main characters, but I have retained sufficient artistic licence to enliven the stories as I interpret them and see fit.

ACKNOWLEDGEMENTS

In writing these stories I was fortunate to have the support of many people. I am grateful for the help of my editors. Nan McNab and Sharon Lapkin's extensive work in editing these stories has been instrumental in making them infinitely better. I have greatly benefitted from their insights, counsel and assistance. They have been remarkably patient with me, nothing was too difficult, and they were a pleasure to work with. I owe a huge debt of gratitude to them for their incredibly generous support. They gave willingly of their time and I have benefitted from their understanding, acumen and direction.

My heartfelt thanks to Bob Sessions for his support and guidance in the writing, editorial and publication process. I have also benefitted from the endless hours of typing, retyping and researching by Noni Carr-Howard.

Finally, many friends have been there for me along this journey. They are too numerous to name—you know who you are. Thank you for your support and encouragement. And last but not least, thank you to my family who have helped me keep everything in perspective.

*For my wife Wendy, daughters Amy and Rachel,
daughter-in-law Deb, son-in-law Joel,
and grandchildren Goldie, Ziggy and Millie.*

CONTENTS

Preface		1
Introduction		4
1.	Rosa Parks	13
2.	Crisis in Little Rock	31
3.	The Greensboro Sit-in	49
4.	The March on Washington	65
5.	The Assassination of Malcolm X	79
6.	Selma to Montgomery March	97
7.	The Assassination of Martin Luther King, Jr	117
8.	Poor People's Campaign, Washington 1968	141
9.	The 1968 Democratic National Convention	157
10.	The Chicago Eight Conspiracy Trial	179
11.	Bring the Troops Home	199
12.	Death of a Revolutionary: George Jackson and the Soledad Brothers	215
13.	The Equal Rights Amendment and Women's Strike for Equality	233

PREFACE

I am a child of the 1960s who came of age during the final years of that tumultuous decade. From far-off Australia, I watched in fascination as the United States was engulfed by a social and political revolution.

Those ten years saw the end of Jim Crow racial segregation, the emergence of the women's liberation and gay rights movements, a series of brutal assassinations, and mass agitation against the Vietnam War. Longstanding social, economic and political conventions were shattered by radical changes to American society that have endured to this day.

Among those concurrent social revolutions of the 1960s, the struggle for civil rights resonated with me most. That decade featured the centennial anniversary of the American Civil War and three 'reconstruction amendments' that were intended to bestow equal citizenship on former slaves. Yet, a full hundred years after the guns fell silent at Appomattox County, Virginia, American blacks still suffered as second-class citizens.

Discriminatory voter registration laws denied the franchise to African Americans, shutting them out from political power. Private businesses routinely denied service to people solely on the basis of race. And, despite the Supreme Court's *Brown v Board of Education* ruling of 1954, thousands of public schools remained racially segregated. In America's South, this regime of bigotry was enforced not only by the local judicial system, but also through terrorist violence inflicted by groups such as the Ku Klux Klan.

Civil rights organisers were murdered in Mississippi. Four young girls aged eleven to fourteen years of age were killed by a bomb planted at an African American church in Birmingham, Alabama. Peaceful protesters were beaten, tear-gassed and mauled by police dogs throughout the South.

The righteousness of the civil rights cause was equalled by the viciousness with which it was opposed. Yet John F Kennedy, with an eye towards his 1964 re-election, was loath to support the cause of racial equality for fear of losing Democratic Party dominance over the so-called 'Solid South'.

Martin Luther King, Jr, and other civil rights leaders understood that the aversion to civil rights reform dominating the American political establishment would only be overcome through the exertion of political pressure. The powers that be in Washington would only legislate change if the pain of maintaining the status quo became more acute than the cost of changing it. Only then would there be any chance of abolishing the outrageous regime of legal bigotry that marginalised America's racial minorities.

I have chosen to tell the story of protest in the 1960s through the medium of historical fiction, a literary genre that employs artistic licence to enliven the stories of past events while adhering to their factual accuracy.

The fictional protagonists who populate these vignettes are eyewitnesses to some of the most salient chapters of the protest movement. They are all set during the 1960s, with the exception of a story that recounts the 1957 Little Rock high school desegregation crisis through the eyes of a young, white teenager.

The moral lessons arising from this turbulent period of American history are eternal. The struggle for the triumph of justice over injustice, the boundaries of expediency in pursuit of a greater good, the imperative to oppose unrighteousness even though you might be personally immune to its evil—these are all issues that are no less salient during the 2020s than they were during the 1960s.

As a student, maths came easily to me and I gravitated towards the study of accounting. Most of my spare time on campus, however, was spent in the company of law and arts students debating the political issues of the day.

My interest in public affairs has remained over time, and I have tried in my own modest way to advance the principles of social equity, ethnic diversity and global peace. To that end, I declared conscientious objector status during the Vietnam War.

Later, I served as treasurer of the Victorian Council of Civil Liberties, now named Liberty Victoria. I also had the privilege of working with civil rights icon Ron Castan AM QC in establishing the Alan Missen Foundation, a body to disseminate information about civil liberties and human rights throughout Australia. In 2000, I began a journey that would last for almost a decade as Treasurer of the Koori Heritage Trust. Their motto, 'Give me your hand my friend', inspired our vision to embed Aboriginal culture and history into the lives of all Victorian people.

Philosopher George Santayana famously said, 'Those who cannot remember the past are condemned to repeat it'. In that spirit, I hope you find these stories both entertaining and enlightening in equal measure.

INTRODUCTION

The civil rights movement was a struggle by black Americans for equal rights under the law. It took place predominantly during the 1950s and 1960s. The Civil War had legally abolished slavery, but black people continued to endure the damaging effects of racism, especially in the South. By the mid-twentieth century, black Americans decided they had experienced more than enough prejudice and violence. They, with many white Americans, mobilised and began to fight for equality.

JIM CROW LAWS

In 1868, the Fourteenth Amendment to the Constitution gave black people equal protection under the law. In 1870, the Fifteenth Amendment granted black Americans the right to vote. Even so, many white Americans (especially those in the South) were unhappy that black people now had equal opportunities, at least in theory.

To marginalise black people and keep them separate from white people, 'Jim Crow' laws were introduced in the South in the late nineteenth century. The term 'Jim Crow' originated when Thomas Dartmouth, a struggling actor otherwise known as Daddy Rice, appeared on stage in 1898 as Jim Crow, a larger-than-life, stereotypical black character. Rice, a white man, wore blackface, darkening his skin with burnt cork. His Jim Crow song-and-dance routine became a huge success, and his Jim Crow character became a standard in minstrel shows. Jim Crow laws refer to the repressive laws and customs used to restrict and limit black rights. They meant black people couldn't use the same public facilities as white people, live in many of the same towns or go to the same schools. Interracial marriage was illegal, and most black people couldn't vote because they were unable to pass voter literacy tests.

Even though Jim Crow laws were not adopted in Northern states, black people still experienced discrimination at work, when they tried to buy a house and when they tried to get an education. Also, laws were passed in some states to limit voting rights for black Americans.

Additionally, Southern segregation gained ground in 1896 when the US Supreme Court declared that facilities for black and white people could be 'separate but equal'.

WORLD WAR II AND CIVIL RIGHTS

Prior to World War II, most black people worked as low-wage farmers, factory workers and domestics. By the early 1940s, most black Americans were not given the better-paying jobs and they were discouraged from joining the military.

After thousands of black people threatened to march on Washington to demand equal employment rights, President Franklin D Roosevelt issued an executive order on 25 June 1941. It opened national defence and other government jobs to all Americans regardless of race, creed, or colour.

Black men and women served in World War II, despite suffering segregation and discrimination during their deployment. The

Tuskegee Airmen broke the racial barrier to become the first black military aviators in the US Army Air Corps and earned more than 150 Distinguished Flying Crosses. Yet many black veterans met with prejudice upon returning home.

As the Cold War began, President Harry Truman introduced a civil rights agenda, and in 1948 issued an executive order to end discrimination in the military.

Rosa Parks

On 1 December 1955, a forty-two-year-old woman named Rosa Parks found a seat on a Montgomery, Alabama, bus.

When a white man got on the bus and could not find a seat in the white section at the front of the bus, the bus driver instructed Parks and three other black passengers to give up their seats. Parks refused and was arrested.

Word of her arrest provoked outrage and support. Black community leaders formed the Montgomery Improvement Association led by Baptist minister, Martin Luther King, Jr.

The Association staged a boycott of the Montgomery bus system lasting 381 days, and on 14 November 1956 the Supreme Court ruled segregated seating on buses was unconstitutional.

Little Rock Nine

In 1954, the civil rights movement gained momentum when the United States Supreme Court made segregation illegal in public schools. In 1957, Central High School in Little Rock, Arkansas, asked for volunteers from all-black high schools to attend the formerly segregated school.

On 3 September 1957, nine black students, known as the Little Rock Nine, arrived at Central High School to begin classes, but were met by the Arkansas National Guard, under orders from Governor Orval Faubus, and a threatening mob. The Little Rock Nine tried again a couple of weeks later and made it inside, but had to be removed for their safety when violence ensued.

Finally, President Dwight Eisenhower intervened and ordered federal troops to escort the Little Rock Nine to and from classes at Central High. However, the students faced continuing harassment and prejudice.

CIVIL RIGHTS ACT OF 1957

Although all Americans had gained the right to vote, many Southern states made it difficult for black citizens. They required prospective black voters to take literacy tests that were confusing, misleading, and nearly impossible to pass.

Wanting to minimise racial tensions in the South, on 9 September President Eisenhower signed the *Civil Rights Act of 1957* into law. It allowed federal prosecution of anyone who tried to prevent someone from voting, and it created a commission to investigate voter fraud.

WOOLWORTH'S LUNCH COUNTER

Even though black Americans had made some gains, they still experienced prejudice in their daily lives. On 1 February 1960, four college students in Greensboro, North Carolina, refused to leave a Woolworth's lunch counter without being served.

Over the next several days, hundreds of people joined their cause in what became known as the Greensboro sit-ins. After some were arrested and charged with trespassing, protesters boycotted all segregated lunch counters until the owners conceded and the original four students were served at the Woolworth's lunch counter where they had first stood their ground.

Their efforts helped launch the Students Nonviolent Coordinating Committee to encourage all students to get involved in the civil rights movement and encourage black voters to register in Mississippi. Young college graduate, Stokely Carmichael, joined the Student Nonviolent Coordinating Committee in 1964. In 1966, Carmichael became the chair of the committee and in one of his many speeches he coined the phrase 'black power'.

FREEDOM RIDERS

On 4 May 1961, thirteen 'freedom riders' (seven black and six white activists) mounted a Greyhound bus in Washington, DC, embarking on a bus tour of the American South to protest segregated bus terminals.

Facing violence from both police officers and white protesters, the freedom riders drew international attention. On Mother's Day 1961, the bus reached Anniston, Alabama, where a mob mounted the bus and threw a bomb into it. The freedom riders escaped the burning bus but were badly beaten. Photos of the bus engulfed in flames were widely circulated.

US Attorney-General Robert F Kennedy negotiated with Alabama Governor John Patterson and the freedom riders resumed their journey under police escort on 20 May, but the police officers left the group once they reached Montgomery, where a white mob brutally attacked the bus. Attorney-General Kennedy responded to the riders and a call from Martin Luther King, Jr, by sending federal marshals to Montgomery.

On 24 May 1961, a group of freedom riders reached Jackson, Mississippi. Though met with hundreds of supporters, the group was arrested for trespassing in a 'whites-only' facility and sentenced to thirty days in jail. Attorneys for the National Association for the Advancement of Coloured People brought the matter to the US Supreme Court, which reversed the convictions. Hundreds of new freedom riders were drawn to the cause, and the rides continued.

In the fall of 1961, under pressure from the Kennedy administration, the Interstate Commerce Commission issued regulations prohibiting segregation in interstate transit terminals.

MARCH ON WASHINGTON

Arguably, one of the most famous events of the civil rights movement took place on 28 August 1963, the March on Washington. It was organised and attended by many civil rights leaders, including Martin Luther King, Jr.

More than 200,000 people of all races congregated in Washington, DC, for the peaceful march, which aimed to force civil rights legislation and establish job equality for everyone. The highlight of the march was King's, 'I have a dream' speech. It instantly became a slogan for equality and freedom.

CIVIL RIGHTS ACT OF 1964

President Lyndon B Johnson signed the *Civil Rights Act of 1964* legislation, initiated by President John F Kennedy before his assassination, into law on 2 July of that year.

King and other civil rights activists witnessed the signing. The law guaranteed equal employment for all, limited the use of voter literacy tests, and allowed federal authorities to ensure public facilities were integrated.

Selma to Montgomery March

On 7 March 1965, the civil rights movement in Alabama took a violent turn as six hundred peaceful demonstrators participated in the Selma to Montgomery march to protest the killing of black civil rights activist, Jimmie Lee Jackson, by a white police officer.

As the protesters neared the Edmund Pettus Bridge, they were blocked by Alabama state and local police sent by Alabama Governor George C Wallace, a vocal opponent of desegregation. Refusing to stand down, protesters moved forward and were beaten and tear-gassed by police, and dozens of protesters were hospitalised.

The entire incident was televised and became known as 'Bloody Sunday'. Some activists wanted to retaliate with violence, but King pushed for non-violent protests and eventually gained federal protection for another march.

Voting Rights Act of 1965

When President Johnson signed the *Voting Rights Act of 1965* into law on 6 August, he took the *Civil Rights Act of 1964* several steps further. The new law banned all voter literacy tests and provided federal examiners in certain voting jurisdictions. It also allowed the attorney-general to contest state and local poll taxes.

Civil Rights Leaders Assassinated

The civil rights movement had tragic consequences for two of its leaders in the late 1960s. On 21 February 1965, former Nation of Islam leader and Organization of Afro-American Unity founder, Malcolm X, was assassinated at a rally.

On 4 April 1968, civil rights leader and Nobel Peace Prize recipient, Martin Luther King, Jr, was assassinated on a hotel balcony. Emotionally charged looting and riots followed, putting even more pressure on the Johnson administration to push through additional civil rights laws.

Fair Housing Act of 1968

The *Fair Housing Act of 1968* became law on 11 April 1968. It prevented housing discrimination based on race, sex, national origin, and religion. It was the final legislative achievement of the civil rights era.

The civil rights movement was an empowering one for black Americans. The efforts of civil rights activists and numerous protesters of all races brought about legislation to end segregation on buses, in schools, and dining facilities. It also brought about legislation to end black voter suppression and discriminatory employment practices and housing practices prejudicial to blacks. Sadly, it was just the beginning of a struggle that continues to this day.

Equal Rights Amendment and Women's Strike for Equality

The Equal Rights Amendment, which sought to prevent discrimination on the basis of sex, was introduced to Congress three years after women won the right to vote in 1920. Almost fifty years later it was approved by the Senate, but failed to be ratified by a majority of states due to a conservative political and religious campaign.

Betty Friedan's vision for a women's strike or march on 26 August 1970 was surpassed when fifty thousand women blocked New York's 5th Avenue during rush hour, and women protested across the country, demanding equal rights, abortion on demand, equal opportunity, and more accessible childcare. The strike raised the profile of feminism, but many of the aims of both the strike and the ERA are still to be achieved.

1. ROSA PARKS

THE MONTGOMERY BUS BOYCOTT AND FREEDOM RIDES

1 DECEMBER 1955

Rosa Parks sat in the living room of her riverfront apartment in Detroit. The weather that January day was typical of Michigan in winter. The sky was overcast. It was cold and there was hail and snow on the ground. Rosa smiled as she read her name in the December 1999 edition of Time magazine. She was in good company. Albert Einstein was on the front cover, and she was named as one of the magazine's most influential people of the twentieth century.

At eighty-six, her long, dark hair was now grey, but her brown eyes still sparkled and her expression, while dignified, still has something cheerful about it, as if she might break into a broad smile at any moment. She now wore an elegant pair of glasses instead of the small, rimless spectacles she'd worn when she first became a household name.

Rosa Parks's fame resulted from a simple gesture of defiance that captured the attention and imagination of the world. On

1 December 1955, she refused to surrender her seat to a white passenger on a segregated bus in Montgomery, Alabama. Her arrest triggered the Montgomery bus boycott, a landmark event in the American struggle for civil rights. After a boycott lasting more than a year, the United States Supreme Court ruled that laws mandating racial segregation on public buses were unconstitutional. This was a major step towards the desegregation of public services throughout the US.

Rosa Parks received many accolades during her life, but within she bore the emotional scars of someone who had been the victim of racial prejudice. None of her inner trauma could be seen when she visited the White House in September 1996 to receive the Presidential Medal of Freedom—America's highest civilian honour—from the hands of President Bill Clinton. The following June, that presidential honour was complemented by the award of the Congressional Gold Medal, the most prestigious award given by the US legislative branch.

During the White House awards ceremony, President Clinton said, 'In so many ways, Rosa Parks brought America home, to our founders' dreams.' Congresswoman Julia Carson described her as 'the mother of the civil rights movement'. Parks was also awarded the Martin Luther King, Jr, Award and the Spingarn Medal by the National Association for the Advancement of Coloured People (NAACP).

Born on 4 February 1913 in Tuskegee, Alabama, Rosa Louise Macaulay entered a world of rigid, racial segregation and discrimination. Her parents—James and Leona—separated when she was just two years old, and she went with her mother to live with her maternal grandparents on a farm in Alabama. Both grandparents had been born into slavery and were strong advocates of racial equality. Rosa later told of watching her grandfather standing guard near their front door with a shotgun whenever the Ku Klux Klan were about.

Pervasive racial prejudice was a constant feature of life for African Americans in the Jim Crow South. Rosa attended a segregated, one-room school in Pine Level, Alabama, that was lacking desks and other basic school supplies. African American students walked to school while, by contrast, the city of Pine Level provided bus transportation for white children to their new school building.

After completing primary school, Leona enrolled Rosa in the Montgomery Industrial School for Girls, also a racially segregated institution. She went on to attend Alabama State Teachers College High School, but was forced to take a leave of absence due to her grandmother's illness and later death. Then, just as Rosa was planning her return to school, her mother also fell ill. Rosa stayed home to care for Leona while her brother, Sylvester, worked as the family's primary wage-earner. She later persevered with her studies, ultimately graduating with a high-school degree in 1934.

She pursued further studies after she met and married Raymond Parks, a barber from Montgomery, Alabama. It was 1932, the depths of the Great Depression and she was nineteen years old. Raymond was an active member of the NAACP. Some years earlier, he had been active in the campaign to free the Scottsboro Boys, the name given by the press to nine African American men framed on false charges of rape. Rosa joined him in the struggle for civil rights, and by 1943 she was secretary of the local Montgomery NAACP. She also took on the role of the chapter's youth leader until 1957.

Many of Montgomery's African American residents were politically organised long before Parks was arrested for refusing to give up her seat. The Women's Political Council was founded in 1946, and was lobbying the city for improved conditions on the buses for a decade before the bus boycott began. Local civil rights leaders chose to capitalise on Parks's arrest to challenge legalised racial segregation.

When Rosa Parks refused the bus driver's instruction on that December day in 1955, it wasn't because she was tired; she later told a friend that she was just tired of giving in. Rosa felt that she deserved equal dignity and shouldn't set her sights lower than anybody else's just because she was black.

This pivotal moment in American history began after a long day at a Montgomery department store where Rosa Parks worked as a seamstress. She boarded the Cleveland Avenue bus for home and took a seat in the first of several rows designated for 'coloured' passengers.

At the time, the Montgomery City Code required that all public transportation be segregated on the basis of race, with drivers required to provide separate, but equal, accommodations for white and black passengers. This was accomplished by reserving the front of the bus for white passengers and restricting African American passengers to the less comfortable back. When an African American passenger boarded the bus, they would pay their fares at the front of the bus, and then get off and board through the rear door.

As the bus Rosa was riding proceeded along its route, it began to fill with white passengers. Eventually, the driver noticed that several white passengers were standing in the aisle for lack of seats. The bus driver stopped and moved the sign separating the two sections back one row. He then ordered four black passengers to give up their seats.

Three of the other black passengers on the bus complied with the driver, but Parks refused. The driver called the police and she was arrested.

This was not Rosa's first encounter with this particular bus driver. Twelve years earlier in 1943, she had paid her fare at the front of the bus he was driving, then exited so she could re-enter through the back door, as required. As she walked through the winter cold towards the back of the bus, the driver pulled away before she could re-board.

This day in December 1955, Rosa Parks was charged with violating Chapter 6, Section 11, of the Montgomery City Code. She was taken to police headquarters, where she was fingerprinted, and a mug shot was taken while she held the number 7053 to her chest. Later that night, she was released on bail.

That same evening, Edward Daniel Nixon, the president of the Montgomery NAACP, put in motion a plan to boycott local city buses. Advertisements were placed in local papers, and handbills were printed and distributed in black neighbourhoods. As news of the boycott spread, other African American leaders joined the struggle. On Sunday 4 December, ministers proclaimed the boycott from the pulpits of African American churches throughout Montgomery. The *Montgomery Advertiser*, the local newspaper of record, published a front-page article on the boycott action.

Members of the African American community were asked to stay off city buses on Monday 5 December 1955—the day of Parks's trial—in protest of her arrest. People were also encouraged to stay home from work or school. As a result, the city's buses ran mostly empty. Some black Montgomerians carpooled and others rode in cabs operated by African Americans. Most of the estimated forty thousand African American commuters in the city at the time opted to walk to work that day, some over a distance of twenty miles. All in all, an estimated ninety per cent of the African American riders stayed off the buses.

When Rosa Parks arrived at the courthouse that morning with her attorney, Fred Gray, she was greeted by a bustling crowd of about five hundred vocal local supporters. Some carried banners that read, 'We Demand Equal Rights Now'. Others read 'White Mobs Must Go' and 'Police Watch While Black Children Are Beaten'.

The crowd waited patiently until Rosa walked out onto the steps of the courthouse half an hour later. Cheers broke out and members of the crowd threw their hands in the air, shouting 'End prejudice now!' She'd been found guilty of violating a local ordinance and was fined $10, as well as a $4 court fee. But that was only the beginning.

That same morning—5 December 1955—a group of leaders from the African American community had gathered at Mt Zion Church to form the Montgomery Improvement Association (MIA). They elected a relative newcomer to Montgomery by the name of Dr Martin Luther King, Jr, as president. The twenty-six-year-old King had come to Montgomery the previous year to serve as pastor of the Dexter Avenue Baptist Church.

The truth is invariably more complicated than the public perception of events. Rosa Parks was not the first African American to challenge segregated bus transport in Montgomery, Alabama. On 2 March of that year, nine months earlier, a fifteen-year-old high-school student named Claudette Colvin refused to give up her bus seat. But because Colvin was unmarried and pregnant, local civil rights leaders in Montgomery thought she would not be suitable as the public face of the desegregation struggle.

In Rosa Parks, the MIA believed they had the perfect person to headline the Montgomery bus boycott effort. They believed the city government would ultimately have no choice but to submit because the local bus system was heavily dependent on African American riders, who made up seventy-five per cent of its clientele.

Initially, the MIA's demands did not include changing segregation laws. Rather, the group began by demanding courtesy, the hiring of black drivers, and a first-come, first-seated policy, with whites entering and filling seats from the front and blacks from the rear. However, a group of five Montgomery women—including Claudette Colvin—had already filed suit against the City of Montgomery to strike down bus segregation laws entirely. The city government resisted these demands.

To ensure the boycott could be sustained, black leaders organised carpools and Montgomery's African American taxi drivers charged only ten cents, the same price as a bus fare, for black customers. The campaign continued for the next thirteen months, severely crippling the finances of Montgomery's municipal transit company.

The segregationist establishment of Montgomery fought back against the boycott in a variety of ways, both legal and brazenly illegal. Insurance for the city taxi system used by African Americans was cancelled. Boycotters were threatened and fired by their white employers. Police arrested black Montgomerians for violating an antiquated law prohibiting boycotts. On one occasion, they charged eighty leaders with violating a law that prevented conspiracies interfering with lawful business without just cause.

While this was happening, a Montgomery busing lawsuit about mistreatment of black women on city buses—*Browder v Gayle*—wound its way through the American judicial system. Fred Gray and Charles D Langford had filed the case on behalf of four African American women, not including Rosa Parks.

In June 1956, the US District Court found that racial segregation laws violated the equal protection clause of the Fourteenth Amendment. The City of Montgomery appealed, but that lower court ruling was upheld at both the Circuit Court of Appeal and Supreme Court. On 13 November 1956, the final judicial word came down—segregation on public transport was illegal under the Constitution of the United States.

The loss of the Browder case, combined with the economic damage suffered by its transit company and downtown businesses, forced the City of Montgomery to end racial segregation on public buses. This brought the boycott to an end on 20 December 1956.

The Montgomery bus boycott went down in history as a huge success. Lasting a total of 381 days, it was one of the largest and most successful mass movements in American history. It also proved to be just one milestone among many on the road to racial equality in the United States, a road paved with fear and washed with blood.

Black churches were burned and bombed. On the evening of 30 January 1956, the home of Reverend Dr Martin Luther King was attacked. King's role as a leading organiser of the bus boycott made him the object of hatred by the Klan and other white supremacists. He was speaking at a nearby church when an unidentified white man pulled up in a car and tossed an explosive onto the porch of his home. The bomb exploded, damaging the house, but inflicting no harm on King's wife, Coretta, who was inside with the couple's three-month-old daughter, Yolanda.

News of the bombing quickly spread, and an angry crowd soon gathered outside King's home. King acted quickly to defuse this combustible situation, urging non-violence as the proper answer to violence. 'I want you to love our enemies,' he reportedly told his supporters. 'Be good to them, love them, and let them know you love them.'

Later that same year, while the boycott was still in effect, another assailant fired a shotgun towards the Kings' home. Martin Luther King and his family continued to be subjected to death threats until he was assassinated in 1968.

One of the most outrageous incidents of attempted intimidation came from the apex of American political power—the Federal Bureau of Investigation or FBI. Beginning in the 1950s, the FBI conducted covert surveillance and a psychological warfare program against groups and individuals deemed subversive by Director J Edgar Hoover. 'Cointel', as the program was called, sent an anonymous letter in 1964 to the home of Martin Luther King. Opened by his wife, Coretta, the letter threatened to expose King's alleged sexual improprieties if he didn't abandon his civil rights activity. King ignored the letter and continued the fight for justice.

Although the buses were now technically integrated, Montgomery continued to maintain racially segregated bus stops. Even worse, snipers began firing into buses, and one shooter shattered both legs of a pregnant African American passenger.

But on 30 January 1957, the Montgomery police arrested seven members of the infamous Ku Klux Klan for acts of violence against the black community. These arrests largely brought an end to the bus-related attacks.

Rosa Parks also paid a personal price for serving as the public face of the Montgomery bus boycott. She lost her job as a tailor's assistant at the Montgomery Fair department store and her husband, Raymond, was pressured to leave his job as a barber at nearby Maxwell Air Force Base.

Even after the boycott ended, the Parks found it difficult to obtain work in the Montgomery area. Rosa was a volunteer for the MIA, but the organisation did not offer her employment, nor did any other civil rights group. It was said that the male leadership was jealous of the amount of media attention she received. It was tall poppy syndrome, Montgomery-Alabama style.

Faced with limited opportunities in Alabama, in 1957 Raymond and Rosa Parks relocated to Detroit where she had family, but life in Michigan proved very difficult. Raymond had to go through retraining before he could receive a barber's licence and Rosa could only find piecework sewing jobs. She then became ill, having an operation for an ulcer that doctors presumed was caused by the stress of the bus boycott. She also underwent surgery to have a throat tumour removed. By July 1960, a feature article in *Jet* magazine described her as a 'tattered rag of her former self—penniless, debt-ridden, ailing with stomach ulcers and a throat tumour, compressed into two rooms with her husband and mother.'

Despite her personal troubles, Rosa Parks remained involved in the struggle for civil rights after moving to Detroit. By the spring of 1961, Raymond was barbering while she was healthy enough to handle steady work as a seamstress at the Stockton Sewing Company. There she put in ten-hour days and was paid seventy-five cents for each apron and skirt she completed.

Rosa admired Martin Luther King, Jr, as a civil rights leader, having worked with him on the bus boycott. Her own views, however, were aligned with the more radical Malcolm X. She disagreed with King's insistence on non-violence at all costs, stating in one interview that self-protection against violence was not actually violence on the part of blacks. Instead, she argued that such tactics were merely self-protection against victimisation by others.

In 1964, she volunteered for John Conyers, Jr's campaign for Michigan's First Congressional District. After winning that seat, Conyers, in turn, hired Rosa as a receptionist and assistant for his Detroit office. She began work in 1965 and remained there until her retirement in 1988. Conyers described Parks as a humble, quiet person, and he told a local newspaper that 'she was always getting invitations to travel to speak, frequently long distances.'

One day, he said, 'she came to me and asked that her pay be reduced because I was letting her go to these engagements.' He added that Rosa Parks was the only person who'd ever worked for him to ask for a pay decrease. He refused her request.

By all accounts, Rosa Parks excelled at her work. She assisted constituents in joining Conyers at a protest over General Motors' decision to close local plants. Most importantly, the job provided a dignified, middle-class wage, including a pension and health insurance.

The legacy of the Montgomery bus boycott for Raymond and Rosa Parks endured long after it was resolved as a matter of law and public policy. Even though the boycott ended in December 1956, hateful missives continued to be sent to Parks into the 1970s. She was accused of being a traitor and of harbouring communist sympathies. Packages containing rotten watermelons and hate mail were delivered to John Conyers's congressional office addressed to her.

The attacks were so venomous that Raymond suffered a nervous breakdown, which today would likely be ascribed to post-traumatic stress syndrome. Yet none of this viciousness was enough to deter Rosa Parks from continuing her work.

The Montgomery bus boycott set in train other campaigns of civil disobedience designed to protest racial discrimination against African Americans. In 1961, the Congress of Racial Equality (CORE) organised so-called 'freedom rides' through the American South. The freedom rides campaign sought to test a 1960 decision by the Supreme Court that segregation of interstate transportation facilities, including bus terminals, was unconstitutional.

Groups of white and African American civil rights activists employed tactics of peaceful non-compliance with racial segregation rules at bus terminals in Alabama, Mississippi and South Carolina. Accompanied by their white counterparts, black freedom riders would occupy random bus seats and use 'whites-only' restrooms, lunch counters and waiting rooms.

These tactics would usually earn the freedom riders an arrest for disorderly conduct and unlawful assembly. They would be taken to the local courthouse, convicted and quickly sentenced to payment of a fine and in some cases to a term in jail. They were often subjected to police brutality during their arrest and, in some cases, faced severe violence from local segregationists.

The original group of thirteen riders—seven African Americans and six whites—underwent a few days' training in Washington. They conducted role-playing exercises to prepare them for a nonviolent response to the harassment they would surely endure.

These freedom riders left Washington, DC, on 4 May 1961, planning to reach New Orleans, Louisiana, two weeks later on 17 May. This would be the seventh anniversary of the US Supreme Court's landmark *Brown v Board of Education* ruling that racial segregation of the nation's public schools was unconstitutional.

The group travelled through Virginia and North Carolina without incident until they reached Rock Hill, South Carolina, on 12 May. Seminary student, John Lewis, who would later lead the Student Nonviolent Coordinating Committee and become a US congressman, was beaten and arrested for the crime of using the whites-only restroom and passenger lounge.

Then on 14 May 1961, a Greyhound bus filled with freedom riders arrived in Anniston, Alabama, where an angry mob of about two hundred white people surrounded the bus. The driver refused to stop, but the mob gave chase in a convoy of cars. Local law enforcement officials had previously promised to turn a blind eye to attacks by the Ku Klux Klan. After stopping to change a slashed tyre, the bus was surrounded by a violent mob armed with baseball bats and iron bars. The freedom riders escaped from the bus as it burst into flames, only to be brutally beaten once outside.

College student, Mae Frances Moultrie, suffered severe smoke inhalation during this incident. She was taken to the hospital along with the other injured freedom riders, but the interracial group was not allowed to spend the night. Moultrie was later quoted as saying she couldn't remember whether she walked or crawled off the bus.

When a second Greyhound bus approached Anniston, eight Klansmen boarded it and beat the freedom riders. The bus managed to press on to Birmingham, Alabama, where the passengers were again attacked at the bus terminal. Birmingham Public Safety Commissioner, Bull Connor, stated that, although he knew the freedom riders were arriving and violence awaited them, he posted no police protection because it was Mother's Day. This was the same Bull Connor who became infamous two years later when he ordered fire hoses and attack dogs to be used against protesting children in the streets of Birmingham.

On 20 May, another vicious race riot occurred when the freedom riders arrived at the bus terminal in Montgomery, Alabama. Later, twenty-one-year-old Catherine Burks described how men, women and children clawed the face of fellow freedom rider, Jim Zwerg.

The following day, an angry segregationist mob laid siege to the African American First Baptist Church in Montgomery. Windows were shattered by rocks, but police were very slow in arriving.

Images of the burning bus and its bloodied passengers were front-page news around the world. Suddenly, the struggle for racial equality in the United States became the topic of global conversation. In a television documentary produced decades later, Christian minister and civil rights activist, Benjamin Elton Cox, described the global impact of this negative publicity, saying that, 'people in Tel Aviv and Moscow and London' were realising for the first time 'that America is not living up to the dream of liberty and justice for all.'

After the violence that occurred during the first wave of freedom rides, bus drivers declined to participate in the program. Then US Attorney-General Robert Kennedy, John Kennedy's brother, took the initiative and negotiated with the governor of Alabama and bus companies to secure both drivers and police protection for freedom riders. When the next Greyhound bus left Birmingham on 20 May, it had a police escort.

Yet the reservoirs of racial bigotry in the South ran deep. The police escort abandoned the freedom riders just before it arrived at the bus terminal in Montgomery, where another angry mob was waiting to attack the activists as they disembarked. Enraged by this blatant breach of his agreement with the Alabama governor, Robert Kennedy dispatched six hundred federal marshals to Montgomery with orders to quell racial violence.

Martin Luther King remained undeterred by segregationist thuggery, organising a service at Montgomery's First Baptist Church the following night. Over a thousand supporters of the freedom riders were in attendance.

But outside the church, another racist mob gathered. Martin Luther King called Robert Kennedy in Washington DC to ask for federal police protection. Kennedy immediately ordered the federal marshals into action, and they used tear gas to disperse the mob. Under pressure from the Kennedy administration in Washington, Governor Patterson finally declared martial law in the city and dispatched the National Guard to restore order.

On 24 May 1961, the freedom riders departed Montgomery for Jackson, Mississippi, where several hundred supporters greeted the arriving bus; but any African American who attempted to use the whites-only facilities was arrested for trespassing and taken to the maximum-security penitentiary at Parchman Farm, Mississippi.

Attorney-General Robert Kennedy issued an official Justice Department statement that same day invoking a 'cooling off' period:

> A very difficult condition exists now in the states of Mississippi and Alabama. Besides the groups of 'Freedom Riders' traveling through these States, there are curiosity seekers, publicity seekers and others who are seeking to serve their own causes, as well as many persons who are traveling because they must use the interstate carriers to reach their destination.
>
> In this confused situation, there is increasing possibility that innocent persons may be injured. A mob asks no questions.
>
> The Alabama and Mississippi law enforcement officials are

meeting the test today, but their job is becoming increasingly difficult.

A cooling off period is needed. It would be wise for those traveling through these two States to delay their trips until the present state of confusion and danger has passed and an atmosphere of reason and normalcy has been restored.

Meanwhile, justice for the freedom riders remained notable for its absence. During one of their trials in Mississippi, the judge turned to face the wall when the freedom riders presented their legal defence. After this outrageous display of judicial bias, the judge went on to sentence the civil rights activists to thirty days in jail. A similar travesty of justice occurred in Tennessee, when protesters were arrested for ignoring the racial segregation of lunch counters. Attorneys from the NAACP Legal Defence Fund appealed those convictions all the way to the US Supreme Court, where they were reversed.

Ongoing violence and arrests directed against civil rights activists in the South continued to garner national and international attention and drew hundreds of new freedom riders to the cause. Ultimately, 436 riders participated in more than sixty rides over the summer of 1961. That autumn, under pressure from the Kennedy administration, the Interstate Commerce Commission issued regulations prohibiting segregation in interstate transit terminals.

The civil rights struggle to desegregate public transportation facilities lasted almost six years from December 1955 until September 1961. It was an important interim step towards racial equality that was finally enacted into law when the *Civil Rights Act of 1964* was signed by President Lyndon Baines Johnson.

Yet as these words are written, the struggle for civil rights in the US remains unfinished. From Portland, Oregon, to Portland, Maine, American citizens of all races, creeds and colours have taken to the streets to demand an end to racism and police brutality.

It is this resilience, this unwillingness of ordinary men and women to accept injustice, that gives us hope for the future.

2. CRISIS IN LITTLE ROCK

4 September 1957

I was a normal kid, a typical product of the what, where and when of my childhood. The 'what' was heterosexual white male. The 'where' was Little Rock, Arkansas. And the 'when' was 1957. By any measure of the social totem pole at that time and place, the serendipity of my birth positioned me at the very top.

Arkansas in the mid-twentieth century was Jim Crow country where blacks were third-class citizens at best. Racial discrimination was engrained throughout every facet of life in this former slave-holding Confederate state. The subservience of blacks was taken for granted and woe betide any negro who might seek to upend that rigid social order.

I later came to recognise just how wrong the racial inequity of the segregationist South was, but I must confess to having played a role in perpetuating that system through cowardice and passivity.

The shame I have always felt doesn't excuse my actions or, to be more precise, my inaction.

Some people say, 'You were young and didn't know any better,' and there is truth to that statement. Yet that truth—and all my subsequent work on behalf of reconciliation—goes only so far in rebalancing the scales of justice in which we are all weighed. Juvenile or not, my character was tested in 1957 and found wanting.

My tenth-grade year had just begun, when I joined a mob outside Central High School to jeer Elizabeth Eckford as she strode up the sidewalk towards the front entrance. Looking back at it now through the prism of six decades, the thing that I most remember, besides my own shameful behaviour, was the dignified demeanour of this fifteen-year-old African American girl. Her black hair was cut short and she wore a neat, white dress with a navy-blue check trim. She held herself tall, looking straight ahead, as she walked towards the building past the screaming crowd. Holding a folder under her left arm, she was doing her best to remain impassive in the face of the hostility around her.

At the time, I never even considered the perspective of that brave girl and other black kids who wanted nothing more than the same education that I took for granted. To my undying shame, on that day I joined the raucous mob of hecklers outside Central High School. And at that moment I became the ugly product of an ugly environment.

This incident took place on Wednesday 4 September, when nine African American students attempted to enter Central High School for the first time. Late on Tuesday evening, the students had been informed by the principal that they would be attending school the next day.

I later read that Daisy Bates, president of the Arkansas NAACP, called the children's parents to brief them on the logistics for the following morning.

'Do not come to school alone,' she reportedly said, 'I've arranged to meet a group of local African Americans and white ministers near the school at 8.30 am. They will escort the students to school.'

The Eckfords were a family of modest means and did not own a telephone. This meant Elizabeth was not aware of the NAACP's changed plan.

The next morning, Elizabeth took the bus to school and I watched as Elizabeth Eckford approached Central High, only to encounter troops from the Arkansas National Guard who had formed a cordon around the building. With their bayonets unsheathed, they refused to let her pass. Very quickly, she found herself in the middle of an angry crowd of over three hundred protesters along Park Street. I know this firsthand because I was part of the mob.

Then, a second black student, Terrence Roberts, approached the school, but he was halted by the same cordon of national guardsmen. Although the crowd also taunted Roberts, it was Elizabeth Eckford who bore the brunt of our racist rage. Chants of 'two, four, six, eight, we don't want to integrate!' rang out. For the first few moments I joined in hurling racist slurs and violent threats. I grinned as people spat on the girl as she made her way to the end of Park Street in the hope of finding refuge at a bus stop.

The next bus wasn't due for thirty-five minutes, which must have seemed like an eternity for Elizabeth, so she sat there, her hands grasped in her lap. She removed her sunglasses at one point, wiped her face clean and then put them back on again.

A middle-aged white man slid onto the bus stop bench beside her. Somebody told me later that he was Benjamin Fine, education editor for the *New York Times*, covering the events. I watched as Fine leaned over to whisper words in Elizabeth's ear. I didn't hear it, but I later learned that he said, 'Don't let them see you cry.'

Then a white woman elbowed her way through the crowd to Elizabeth's side. 'She's scared!' the woman shouted at the mob as her face creased in righteous rage. 'She's just a young girl. Six months from now you'll be ashamed of what you're doing!'

'Go home! You're just one of them niggah-lovers!' a member of the mob shouted at her. I didn't know the woman who defended Elizabeth, but it turned out she was a Little Rock resident by the name of Grace Lorch.

I watched as Mrs Lorch escorted Elizabeth to the other side of the street, but the crowd followed.

'Won't somebody please call a taxi?' she pleaded. The only response from the mob was more taunts.

As I look back now, I see that this bus stop incident was the beginning of my metamorphosis from darkness to light. Despite the principles of my upbringing, spoken and unspoken, despite the racist social order that I had always taken for granted, I began to feel a visceral distaste for the brutal bullying taking place before my eyes.

To my everlasting shame and subsequent regret, I didn't possess the moral courage to take a stand there and then. Instead, I stood there, a silent onlooker as the baying mob browbeat a young girl and the woman protecting her. Yes, I was a child myself, but I am not inclined to make such allowances for myself.

In any event, Mrs Lorch and Elizabeth worked their way through the jostling, jeering crowd around the corner into West 14th Street where they saw a bus approaching. Mrs Lorch flagged it down. As the duo clambered onto the bus, I was struck by how the fifteen-year-old showed her character by simply retaining her sense of dignity. Members of the rabble were so blinded by hatred they could not recognise how they were diminished by each curse and insult they uttered.

It was clear there would be no school that day. Even if classes were conducted, I was in no state of mind to sit quietly for forty-five-minute periods until late afternoon. Besides, I had more serious matters to ponder.

I went home, where I kept my thoughts to myself. I said nothing when my father voiced his approval of the decision by Governor Orval Faubus to deploy the Arkansas National Guard at Central High. I remained quiet when my brothers spewed invective against the damned 'New York commies', coming down to meddle in our Arkansas business.

Then, I began to read, everything I could get my hands on, including newspapers, *Time* and *Newsweek*, and even *The Nation*, when I could find a copy in the Little Rock Public Library.

This is how I learned about the story of that day from the other side, from the perspective of those on the receiving end of the mob's abuse.

I read Elizabeth Eckford's account of her ordeal, in which she spoke about the terrible feeling of being alone and not knowing whether she would ever make it out, and of the deafening roar closing in around her and her fear of being injured.

The *New York Times* featured a story by Benjamin Fine, who wrote, 'Here she is this little girl, this tender little thing, walking with this whole mob baying at her like a pack of wolves seeking to destroy a little lamb.' I later learned that he was the brave soul who sat down beside Elizabeth Eckford that day in defiance of the mob.

According to news accounts, the remaining eight black students arrived after 8 am at the corner of Park and 13th streets as originally planned by Daisy Bates. Joining them were local African American children and white clergymen who escorted them to school. Terrence Roberts and Melba Pattillo walked separately to school.

As this mixed group of students and clergy approached Central High School, they encountered the same segregationist mob and the cordon of national guardsmen. Dunbar Ogden, president of the Greater Little Rock Ministerial Association, acted as spokesman for the group. When he approached the guard, he was met by Lt Colonel Marion Johnson, the commanding officer of the National Guard detachment.

Colonel Johnson told the group that he wasn't authorised to admit any black students. On orders from Governor Faubus, he told them, they were to be denied entry to Central High School. He then signalled a point beyond which they weren't permitted to go.

Many white students had been threatening a walkout if the black students were allowed into Central High School. Now that they saw that the old segregationist regime was being maintained at bayonet point by the Arkansas National Guard, the white students began to attend their classes as if nothing had occurred. An aura of anticlimax settled over the scene and the crowd began to disperse,

At a press conference held that evening, Governor Faubus boasted about deploying the National Guard to preserve the racial segregation of Central High School. In response to questions from journalists, Faubus denied that his actions were in violation of federal law. He argued that his paramount responsibility as governor was to maintain public peace and order. In his judgement—he said—there was a real danger of disorder and violence, and of people inflicting bodily harm on others.

Of course, the verdict of law and history holds that the actions of Orval Faubus were illegitimate. In its groundbreaking case of *Brown v Board of Education* ruling four years earlier, the United States Supreme Court had declared that the 'separate but equal' doctrine used to justify racial segregation in schools was unconstitutional.

But in defiance of the *Brown* decision, segregationist governments throughout the South adopted a Fabian—perhaps better termed 'Faubusian'—strategy of playing for time. Little Rock School superintendent, Virgil Blossom, announced his intention to comply with the Supreme Court decision, but only after an implementation decree was issued.

These delaying tactics were unacceptable to the NAACP, which filed suit in an effort to force the hand of recalcitrant school districts throughout the United States. The following May, the Supreme Court ordered that school desegregation plans should be implemented 'with all deliberate speed'.

But state governments throughout the Jim Crow South still refused to comply, exploiting the lack of a specific time frame in the court's decision to continue their foot-dragging strategy. In Little Rock, the school board adopted an incremental desegregation program over six years that came to be called the 'Blossom Plan'.

The NAACP was disinclined to wait any further and decided to force the issue. In January 1956, twenty-seven black students were refused enrolment by the Little Rock School District. The following month, the NAACP Legal Defense Fund filed suit in the federal court asking for immediate desegregation of Little Rock's public school system.

Two months later, in March 1956, Arkansas's two senators and six congressmen, all Democrats, signed a *Declaration of Constitutional Principles*, a document known in common parlance as the *Southern Manifesto*. The manifesto accused the Supreme Court of abusing its power and vowed to resist desegregation. It was ultimately signed by 101 senators and congressmen from states of the former Confederacy, of whom ninety-nine were Democrats.

Then in August 1956, the US District Court for the Eastern District of Arkansas upheld Little Rock's incremental desegregation plan, declaring that the local school board was acting in 'utmost good faith'. The NAACP appealed to the Eight Circuit Court of Appeals in St Louis, which upheld the lower court ruling.

The next move in the state of Arkansas's strategy of delay was a law that waived attendance requirements for children in integrated public schools. A pro-segregation community organisation called the 'Capital Citizens Council' petitioned Governor Faubus to maintain the regime of racial separation in Little Rock public schools. The council also sent letters to the Little Rock School Board making the same request. Superintendent Blossom responded by declaring that the federal courts had left him no choice, but promised that Central High was the only school in the system that would be opened to black students. However, even this grudging concession to the Supreme Court was enough to enrage the diehard segregationists of Little Rock.

The smouldering embers of racism burst into flame three weeks later, on Monday 23 September. That morning, I arrived at Central High to see another belligerent mob gathered outside the Park Street entrance to the building. This time there were close to one hundred police officers who were facing off against what appeared to be a far larger crowd of angry white folk.

Going by the shouts and curses from members of the crowd, I learned that nine black students had entered the school through a side door. Soon, words shifted into action as the mob went on a rampage. Windows were smashed with rocks and rioters began to fight with police.

Amid this unfolding chaos, I saw four African American men cross the street and approach the police line.

'What's your business here?' I heard a policeman ask.

I later learned the men were Alex Wilson of the *Memphis Tri-State Defender,* James Hicks of the *Amsterdam News,* and Moses J Newson of the *Baltimore Afro-American.* One of the men flashed his press credentials.

I followed the policeman's eyes as he glanced at the approaching mob. Two white men moved around and spread their arms to block the path of the African American journalists.

'Get out of here,' one of the white people yelled. 'Go home, you son of a bitch!'

One of the reporters—Alex Wilson—was nicely dressed in a dark-grey suit, red tie and tan fedora hat. His response to the belligerent challenge from the mob was just as classy as his dress. 'We're newspapermen,' he replied in a calm voice. 'We're just here to do our jobs.'

'You'd better leave,' interjected the policeman nervously. The reporters moved to the left, but the crowd of angry whites matched the journalists' movements. I watched as the policeman suddenly walked away and members of the mob engulfed the three reporters and subjected them to kicks and blows.

Once again, I stood in silent terror, too much of a coward to intervene. I watched in dismay as Earl Davey received a vicious shove to the chest.

'You'd better leave,' barked a member of the mob.

Another protester bellowed, 'You'd better watch what you write.'

Soon I saw the four black journalists retreating to the other side of the street while dodging blows and kicks from the mob. My relief at seeing them apparently escape serious injury was soured by my self-loathing over my failure to intervene.

That evening I watched the CBS television news and learned that Little Rock Mayor, Woodrow Mann, had sent a telegram to the White House. Mann warned the president that the mob outside Central High School posed a serious danger to lives and property in Little Rock.

I slept badly that night. The next morning, I walked into the kitchen to find my father fuming at the news in the *Arkansas Democrat-Gazette*.

'Damned Yankees,' he cursed. 'Always meddling in our business.'

'Who, Dad?' I asked.

'The damned president, that's who. The bastard went and issued one of those proclamations calling for us to let negroes into our schools.'

I didn't want to provoke my father by pointing out that Dwight Eisenhower was from Kansas, not Massachusetts or New York. So, I simply asked if I could see that morning's paper.

'Well, I have to get to work, anyway,' he growled, passing the *Democrat-Gazette* to me. 'Are you going to school today?'

'If I can,' I replied, 'but not if there's going to be more rioting.'

My father nodded and left the kitchen. Moments later I heard the front door close.

With my father gone, I turned my attention to the newspaper and read how Eisenhower had issued a presidential proclamation that denounced 'unlawful assemblages' and 'conspiracies' surrounding the enrolment of black students at Central High.

I attended class that day, avoiding the mob assembled outside Central High by entering through a side door. That evening I watched Walter Cronkite on the CBS News announce that Mayor Mann had sent another message to President Eisenhower pleading for federal intervention. The mob was armed and engaging in fisticuffs, he said. Then he warned about other acts of violence, and said the situation was out of control with police not able to disperse the rioters.

Towards the end of the news broadcast, Cronkite announced that President Eisenhower would be delivering a special address to the nation at 9 pm that night.

I sat with my parents and siblings in front of the television as the president announced the federalisation of the Arkansas National Guard and the dispatch of paratroopers from the 101st Airborne Division to Little Rock. As the president spoke, those paratroopers were already in position at Central High.

I kept my joy a secret as my family complained bitterly about tyrants in Washington sticking their noses into our local affairs, and I watched with quiet satisfaction the next morning—Wednesday 25 September—when nine black students were escorted through the front doors of Central High School by a platoon of soldiers with rifles at the ready. As Elizabeth Eckford and her friends walked up the path towards the school building, I could see the tension in their faces. Although, with a battalion of army paratroopers posted around the school's perimeter, they had little cause for worry.

I cast a glance of contempt towards a crowd of students outside the building who were chanting 'two, four, six, eight, we ain't gonna integrate.' Then I looked at the soldiers and smiled.

An outer cordon of more paratroopers was posted three blocks from the school, and for the first time since school began three weeks earlier, mobs were nowhere to be seen outside Central High School.

At 10 am we were ushered into the auditorium for a special school assembly. Instead of our principal, we were addressed by an army officer who introduced himself as Major General Edwin Walker. General Walker told us in no uncertain terms that the US Army would guarantee that nobody was going to interfere with children coming and going from school in pursuit of their studies.

I noticed that there were fewer students in the auditorium that day than usual. It turned out that 750 of Central High's two thousand students had stayed away from school.

This act of boycott by segregationist students and their families did little to halt the progress of dismantling Jim Crow segregation in Arkansas. An order mandating the integration of all high schools in Little Rock was soon handed down by the Federal District Court.

That night, Governor Faubus appeared on television to decry the tyranny of the federal government and to announce that Arkansas was now occupied territory.

'What an asshole,' I muttered.

'Language!' said my mother.

My father cast a baleful look in my direction. 'Are you saying that you're siding with these Yankee carpetbaggers coming down here to tell us how to live?'

I felt strangely calm as I returned my father's glare and said, 'I think President Eisenhower is doing the right thing. I think our schools should be integrated.'

'Go to your room,' my father thundered. As I rose from the couch, I was beyond fear. I felt liberated from the petty prejudices of my father, along with the crude bigotry of the small-minded men who were trying to retain the evil that was Jim Crow. At the time I didn't know that I had sown the seeds of estrangement from my father. But, even if I had, the need to take a stand against injustice made it a price I had to pay.

Paratroopers of the 101st remained in Little Rock for precisely one month. The nine students entered Central High's front door for the first time without an escort by federal troops on 24 October 1957. That day I watched as they walked along the path towards the front door.

The job of protecting the Little Rock Nine, as those black students were now known, from harassment and bullying within Central High fell to Vice-Principal Elizabeth Huckaby. She did her best, but her best fell unfortunately short of perfection.

I once saw Mrs Huckaby confront a large group of white students who were harassing black students outside the building. On another occasion a group of white students burned an African American effigy. More than once the school authorities were forced to suspend students and, by the third week of school, every black student was assigned two guards for their protection.

The violence, threats and abuse continued unabated. In November, one of the nine was struck by a white student and another was insulted and pushed while leaving a school assembly. Threats of boycott were made against *Arkansas Gazette* because of the newspaper's editorial stand in favour of integration.

I particularly recall one instance when one of the nine fought back. A girl by the name of Minnijean Brown dumped chilli over the heads of two white boys who'd been bumping into her with their chairs as she walked through the cafeteria. Minnijean was suspended for two days, then on her return to school a group of white students dumped their lunch on Minnijean. This incident resulted in the white students' suspension.

Far more worrisome were the bomb threats received at the

school, especially when one of them culminated in a cache of dynamite being discovered in an unused locker.

Yet those nine brave students persevered and on Tuesday 27 May 1958, Ernest Green became the first African American student to graduate from Central High School.

There were points of light during this period for me as well. On 12 October 1957, I defied my father again by attending a service at Immanuel Baptist Church to pray for a peaceful resolution of the crisis. The service was part of a mass prayer program involving thousands of worshippers who came together at churches and synagogues throughout the city of Little Rock.

Dyed-in-the-wool segregationist Governor Faubus continued to make trouble whenever and wherever he could. He spread false rumours that the paratroopers of the 101st Airborne Division had invaded the privacy of the girls' dressing rooms at Central High. On 15 September 1958, he ordered the closure of four Little Rock high schools pending the outcome of a public referendum on desegregation, in blatant defiance of Supreme Court rulings. A week later, white citizens of Little Rock gave Faubus just the excuse he needed to keep the city's public high schools closed. They voted 19,470 to 7,561 against integration. The schools would remain closed for almost an entire calendar year.

Amid the displays of bigotry, there were growing signs that decency would ultimately prevail. When the Little Rock School Board failed to renew the contracts of forty-four pro-integration teachers and administrators in May 1959, members of the community rose up to protest. A group called The Women's Emergency Committee to Open Our Schools (WEC) was formed, joining with local business leaders to conduct a petition for the recall of three overtly racist school board members. Under the catchy acronym STOP (Stop This Outrageous Purge) the recall campaign succeeded in dismissing the three racists from the school board, replacing them with moderates. It was this reconstituted Little Rock School Board that voted to reopen the city's high schools on 12 August 1959.

That same day, a group of segregationists rallied at the State Capitol when Orval Faubus came out of his office to address them. Faubus referred to it as a dark day and urged the crowd to keep up the struggle. The rowdy racists took the governor's words to heart and they marched to Central High where the police and fire departments soon broke up the crowd. I watched the melee from my classroom window and read in the next day's newspaper that twenty-one people had been arrested.

Harry Ashmore, the editor of the *Arkansas Gazette*, said of the crisis in Little Rock: 'Orval Faubus was the hero to the mob; the nine courageous black children he failed to keep out of Central High were the heroes to the world.'

It has been said that the riot of 12 August 1959 was the last spasm of Jim Crow segregation in the state of Arkansas. Looking back now through the prism of a forty-five-year career as an educator, the story isn't quite that simple.

It is true that formal, state-enforced racism began to fade from Arkansas society under pressure from the Civil Rights Division of the US Justice Department. However, changes in public law enforced from above usually do not mirror changes in private hearts. Orval Faubus continued to win elections by large margins before finally leaving the governor's mansion in January 1967.

I suppose this reality informed the course of my own life. I wanted to do my bit to help make Arkansas a place of pride, rather than shame. The best way to achieve this, I concluded, was by teaching. After graduating from Central High, I was awarded a scholarship to Vanderbilt University in Nashville, Tennessee, where I studied history. From there I went on to complete my MA and PhD at Duke University in North Carolina. I chose the Central High saga as the topic of my doctoral dissertation.

A fortunate high number in the draft lottery enabled me to sidestep direct involvement in the Vietnam War. By mid-1969, I was an assistant professor of history at Arkansas State University. Five books and a few dozen peer-reviewed journal articles earned me respect as a serious scholar of civil rights history. Over the years that reputation for scholarship generated several job offers at more prestigious universities, but I remained where I was. My commitment to local change, which arose out of what I witnessed at Central High that year, remained undiminished.

I would like to report that my relationship with my family endured the tensions that erupted during the Central High crisis. In truth, our different values destroyed whatever sense of affection had existed between us. My father and brothers remained firm supporters of Jim Crow; the only change I observed in them was that, as time passed, they kept their bigotry more to themselves.

For my mother, a woman of traditional background, open defiance of her husband was unthinkable. On those rare occasions when we met, I thought I could detect a quiet yearning in her eyes. However, as our estrangement deepened over the years, she adhered to the rules of my excommunication from the family, as dictated by my father.

I did not attend his funeral. After his death I was able to reconcile with my mother for the final few months of her life. The last time I encountered my brothers was at my mother's gravesite. I have had no contact with them over the decades since.

Now, as my retirement nears, I gaze out at the faces staring back at me in the classroom, noting the variety of races, genders, faiths and sexual orientations. This diversity affords me considerable comfort. It is not that America is perfect. Far from it. There is always more to do, but there's also no denying we've come a long way as a culture and a society.

If I have played a minor role in that evolution, within the local ambit of my influence, I am grateful. The price I paid for my moral convictions was any semblance of a relationship with my family. Yet, in retrospect, given who they were and what they believed, I would have struggled to spend time in their company anyway.

My sense of satisfaction over whatever I may have accomplished is underpinned by a resolve to continue the struggle for racial equity as long as my life and health permit.

3. THE GREENSBORO SIT-IN

1 FEBRUARY 1960

I shivered, putting my hand up to my head as the gusting winter wind threatened to abscond with my favourite hat. It was the forest-green beret I'd picked up the previous year during my semester abroad in Paris as a French lit. major.

But I digress.

That first day of February 1960, I slipped through the doors of Woolworths on Elm, breathing a sigh of relief as the heated interior thawed my stiff muscles. I suppose it's true that we North Carolinians don't handle cold weather well.

Sliding the beret into my coat pocket, I made my way through the store towards the lunch counter, yearning for a hot fudge sundae. The aroma of freshly cooked food was my guide as I wended my way through the racks of small jackets in the boys clothes section.

I entered the restaurant section of the store, only to be confronted by a sight sufficiently unusual to stop me in my tracks. This was Greensboro, North Carolina, and I'd never seen anything like the four neatly- dressed, young black men sitting in quiet defiance at the lunch counter marked 'Whites Only'.

They appeared urbane and well-educated, most probably students from the local black college, North Carolina A&T, whereas I was a senior at the Woman's College of the University of North Carolina, colloquially known as the WC.

A tense silence had settled over the counter, broken only by the tinkle of cutlery as people put aside their meals to watch the drama as it unfolded.

'Could we be served, please?' I heard one of the four ask in a polite tone.

'Y'all know the rules,' replied the white waiter from behind the counter. 'Those seats are for whites only. Blacks are served standing up. So, it's time for y'all to move.'

The other restaurant customers looked on in silent fascination as the quartet remained seated.

One of the four, the leader perhaps, said in a voice that resonated with calm determination, 'You've served us already and we can prove it. We have receipts.' He removed a toothbrush, toothpaste and soap from a brown paper bag and placed the items on the counter along with a printed receipt. 'We bought all these things here in the store, and now we just want to be served like everyone else.'

'But you ain't everyone else,' said the soda jerk. 'You can shop here, but you can't eat here. So, it's time for you to move.'

An apron-clad black man in his fifties, with a weathered face and tired eyes, emerged from the kitchen and approached the defiant quartet.

'Why don't you jus' git before ya make trouble for the rest of us?' the man pleaded. 'This ain't the way to bring change.'

'It's the only way,' replied one of the four, accentuating his refusal to move with a decisive shake of the head.

An overweight white man, who looked to be in his forties,

entered the restaurant area. 'I'm Clarence Harris, the store manager. I'm gonna give you a chance to rethink what you're doin' before trouble comes down on yo heads.'

The four young men gazed up at Harris in silence. They did not move.

'All right,' said the manager. 'You asked for it and now you're gonna get it. I'm callin' the police.'

Harris disappeared, only to return ten minutes later accompanied by a Greensboro police officer. The officer pulled a truncheon from his belt and began pacing along the counter just behind the seated young men, slapping the billy club against his hand. The four young men remained seated, eyes front, ignoring this obvious effort at intimidation.

Just then, an elderly white woman stood up and walked over to the four.

'Hello, my name is Cynthia Partridge,' she said with a hand extended in greeting.

'Franklin McCain,' replied the most vocal member of the group, shaking the offered hand.

'And who are your friends?' asked Partridge.

McCain smiled. 'Ezell Blair, David Richmond and Joseph McNeil.'

McCain's three companions nodded in acknowledgement.

'I'm pleased to make your acquaintance, but I have to confess to being a bit disappointed.'

McCain's face creased in a quizzical expression. 'Disappointed, ma'am? Why are you disappointed in us for simply asking to be served like everyone else?'

I saw the woman place her hand on Joseph McNeil's shoulder and say, 'I'm disappointed it took you so long.'

'Ma'am, you shouldn't get yourself involved in this trouble,' advised the policeman in a tone of warning.

I couldn't stand by any longer. 'What trouble, officer?' I interjected while moving to stand between Mrs Partridge and Franklin McCain.

The cop's face creased in a grimace of perplexed annoyance.

I decided to retain the initiative. 'Racial discrimination in schools was abolished by the Supreme Court in its Brown decision six years ago. These people are simply demanding equal treatment under the law.'

The policeman shrugged and walked over to confer with the store manager.

After several moments of whispered discussion, Clarence Harris made an announcement in a loud voice. 'I'm sorry, ladies and gentlemen. The restaurant will be closing early today. Please pay your bills and leave.'

'I'm very proud of you, dear,' Mrs Partridge said to me.

I felt my cheeks redden. 'It was nothing.'

'No, it wasn't,' said Joseph McNeil. 'You stepped into a struggle that wasn't yours to fight. And that's ...'

'Sorry,' I interrupted, 'but I have to disagree. "Whatever you did for the least of these brothers and sisters of mine you did for me." Not that you are least by any measure.'

'Matthew 25:40,' smiled Franklin McCain. 'I see you know your scripture.'

'I try,' I replied.

'Black lover!' spat one of the restaurant patrons as he left.

'Lover of humanity, sir,' I replied to the bigot's retreating back. I turned back to McCain. 'Sorry.'

'For what? We're responsible for our own actions, no one else's.'

I extended my hand. 'Josie Stanton. I'm a senior majoring in French at the WC.'

'Franklin McCain,' he said, giving my hand a polite shake. 'Freshman at A&T.'

'I was hoping for a hot fudge sundae,' I grinned. 'I suppose that will to have to wait.'

McCain grinned. 'Perhaps I should be the one apologising.'

I laughed. 'A bit of ice cream and chocolate is a small price to pay for doing what's right.'

An awkward pause ensued before I broke the silence.

'I have to get to class,' I said, as I pulled the beret onto my head. 'Perhaps I'll see you around.'

'Perhaps,' McCain replied.

The following day, the campus was abuzz with the news of the Woolworths sit-in. I was studying in the Jackson Library when I heard an indignant voice at a nearby table.

'Those uppity blacks. Why change the way things have always been done? They've got their place and we've got ours.'

I turned in my chair. It was a girl I'd seen around campus, but had never met. 'Maybe we're overdue for a change. Besides, racial segregation was declared illegal by the Supreme Court in 1954.'

She glared. 'They're holding another one of those sit-ins at Woolworths right now. If you feel so strongly about it, why don't you go and get yourself arrested with the other riffraff.'

'Thanks for the information,' I replied. 'I was there yesterday and if there's another sit-in going on now, I'd best be going.'

As I rose from my seat, I heard the intake of breath behind me. I adjusted my beret at what I hoped was a jaunty angle, gave a snort of contempt and strode out of the library.

It was just over a mile from the Woman's College campus

to Elm Street and as I approached Woolworths, I saw a couple of television cameras on the sidewalk outside. Pushing my way through the doors into the restaurant area, I saw that the sit-in had grown to around two dozen.

I waved hello to Franklin McCain and received a friendly smile in response. He beckoned me to approach and I slid into a vacant booth.

'I can see you have a nose for trouble,' he grinned.

'What is it they say about nothing ventured?' I replied, with a grin of my own. 'So, what do you think? Are we going to jail?'

McCain shrugged. 'Don't know. But it won't be too bad because of that.' He indicated a TV news crew that was filming the sit-in with a tilt of his head.

'Sunlight is the best disinfectant,' I replied, 'or so said Louis Brandeis.'

McCain nodded in agreement and we began to chat. I learned that he was from Lexington, North Carolina, and was the first of his family to attend college. He planned to major in chemistry followed by medical school, or so he hoped.

In turn, I told him of my hopes of using my degree in French as a springboard to study at the Sorbonne in Paris.

'I've never been outside North Carolina,' he joked, and then the manager, Clarence Harris, announced the premature closing of the restaurant for the second day running.

'We'll be back,' some of the protesters called as they walked out of Woolworths into Elm Street.

And so they were, in even greater numbers. By the next day enough people had joined the sit-in that they occupied almost every seat in the restaurant.

The daily exponential spread of the protest continued, with the glare of news crew camera lights serving as a deterrent against too much police brutality.

This was my final semester before graduation and I had to juggle my classroom assignments and the protests carefully. I was fortunate to find that Madame Fôreter, my academic supervisor, and a senior lecturer in French in the Department of Modern Languages, was supportive.

'*Eet* is a brave thing that you are doing,' she said in her heavy Provençal accent. '*Eet* is always the young who try to change *ze* world.'

'*Merci*, madame,' I rose from my seat and strode out of her office to take part in what had by now become a daily event.

What I didn't expect on the fifth day of the sit-in was a group of white men with belligerent expressions occupying most of the seats in the restaurant.

'Let me,' I whispered to Franklin, who nodded and passed the word to the other protesters.

'Good morning,' I said to the white men in a cheery tone of voice. 'I hope there won't be any problems if we sit down to eat.'

'What's a white girl like you doing with a bunch of radical commie blacks,' growled one, a heavy-set man in his thirties whose battered ears and facial scars gave him the look of a bar brawler.

I ignored him. 'My friends and I simply want to eat a meal in peace.'

'Your friends?' echoed the bar brawler, his voice laden with sarcasm. 'What would your papa say if he knew you were hanging out with them?' he said, with a contemptuous gesture towards the other protesters.

'We don't want any trouble, sir,' said Franklin in a calm voice.

'Then you should take your black ass and that black-loving woman outta here,' the man bellowed, pointing at me.

A quintet of Greensboro police officers suddenly appeared, shouldering their way through the crowd.

'I'm going to have to ask everyone to leave,' announced a cop with sergeant's chevrons on his sleeves. 'Restaurant's closing early.'

We turned to depart and, once outside, Franklin climbed onto a bench to address the crowd of protesters that by now numbered over a hundred.

'Remember our creed of non-violence,' he said in a loud voice. 'If they go low, we stay high. There are other places we can make our presence felt. Let's move to Kress. It's just down the street.'

Franklin took me aside. 'Are you all right?' he asked?

'It's no matter,' I shrugged. 'He was just a nasty, ignorant man.'

But beneath my apparent nonchalance I was quite shaken. The man had radiated violence, and the whole confrontation was unlike anything I had previously experienced. Until this point, I had lived the cosseted life of a white doctor's daughter who had grown up in an affluent suburb of Charlotte.

But I was undeterred.

When we arrived at Kress department store, we found the doors locked. The protesters soon began to disperse and I decided to return to the library and make the most of my time.

Over the following months of my final college semester, I continued to participate in the Greensboro protests. The movement spread, with lunch counter sit-ins cropping up in nearby Winston-Salem then Richmond, Virginia; Nashville, Tennessee; and Atlanta, Georgia.

We were pleased when in March, President Eisenhower at Camp David made an informal comment of support of those struggling for their civil rights. It was an oblique statement that lacked any specific mention of the Greensboro sit-ins, but we took it as an encouraging sign, nonetheless.

Over those weeks and months of winter–spring 1960, Franklin McCain and I became good friends. He was the first black person I'd ever gotten to know on personal terms. Looking back, there's no doubt that the embers of mutual attraction were alight; but this was the American South in the year 1960. Neither he nor I was courageous enough to take that particular plunge.

I graduated in mid-May of 1960 and three weeks later landed at Orly in Paris to take up a one-year position as an English teacher at the Lycée Jean Dautet in La Rochelle.

Even from a distance of four thousand miles I followed the sit-in struggle through the pages of *Le Figaro*, the *International Herald Tribune* and the occasional copies of *Time* and *Newsweek* that came my way.

It was through those pages in July that I learned Woolworths finally integrated its lunch counter after losing hundreds of thousands of dollars in revenue. According to the *Trib*, the manager invited several black restaurant workers to sit at the counter and order food. Even from an ocean away, I felt a measure of satisfaction over my small role in the drama.

I ended up spending just over eight years in France. Twelve months in La Rochelle, followed by a masters at the Sorbonne and a job at UNESCO. By the time I returned to the US, I was accompanied by my French husband and our toddler.

We settled in Manhattan, where I continued my UN work at the headquarters in Turtle Bay, while my husband André began a post-doc research position in the chemistry department at Columbia.

It was a time of terrible social ferment. The Paris we had left behind was convulsed by the student uprising of March 1968. The sixty-eighters, as that generation of protesters became known, built barricades along the streets of the Latin Quarter where they engaged in running battles with police.

The America we found on our arrival was little better. Controversy over the Vietnam War was at its height, with protest marches and draft-card burnings seemingly every week. Martin Luther King, Jr, had been assassinated that April and Robert Kennedy murdered in June. The social fabric of the nation seemed torn asunder.

Like most people, we simply got on with our lives—work and children, saving up to buy rather than rent, and moving our possessions from the apartment building in the East Village to our own brownstone in Brooklyn Heights. The memories of the Greensboro sit-in faded into the background of my daily routine, until one evening some years later when, after putting the girls to bed, André and I sat down to an evening of relaxation in front of the television. But it was not to be.

I was flicking through the channels when I heard the words 'Greensboro sit-in'. I switched back one channel and saw a panel discussion that was broadcast to mark the tenth anniversary of the civil rights protest.

One of the panellists was Julian Bond, a member of the Georgia state legislature who was a rising star in the civil rights movement. I listened as Bond recounted how the civil rights movement began for him on 4 February 1960 while reading a newspaper in the company of a friend.

As Bond told it, when he saw a newspaper headline about the Greensboro sit-in, he pondered whether something similar could be done in Atlanta. When his friend replied with a blasé statement that surely someone would do it, Bond put down the newspaper and asked why shouldn't that someone be us?

I looked over at my husband and whispered, 'I was there.'

André turned to me with a quizzical expression. 'Where were you, darling?' He always addressed me in English to improve his facility with that language.

'At Greensboro.'

'Are you telling me that you played a part in *zose* sit-ins?' he asked, his obvious surprise making his French accent particularly marked.'

'Yes, honey, but only a small part.'

André turned around on the sofa and gazed into my eyes as he took my hands in his. 'It's not the size of the part you played that's important. It's that you made the decision to get involved. You're amazing and you'll have to tell me all about it ... afterwards.'

He held me, and I'll leave the subsequent events to your imagination, making this, perhaps, an appropriate point to conclude the story of my modest contribution to the cause of civil rights ... except for one loose end that needs to be tied off; the question whether Franklin McCain and I ever met again.

The answer is yes—precisely ten years later, on 1 February 1980 at the ceremony of the Greensboro sit-in's twentieth anniversary. To this day, I don't know who tracked me down and how, although I suspect Franklin had something to do with it despite his fervent denials. In any event, in mid-September 1979 a formal invitation on an embossed letterhead appeared in our mailbox asking me to attend the ceremony as an honoured guest.

'Mom, can we go?' asked my eldest daughter, Alice, when I mentioned the invitation at the dinner table that evening. 'We're studying the civil rights movement in civics, and this would be a great story for my class project.'

André and I exchanged glances and smiled.

'I'm sure that no other student in seventh grade will have anything that can match it,' he said.

I nodded. 'No one can deny its educational value. So, I think we should make a family road trip of it.'

'Really, Mom?' said Alice.

'Really,' I confirmed, 'I'll write a note to both your teachers. The ceremony is on a Friday. So, if we leave Wednesday morning, that'll give us two days to get there and we can be back on Sunday night.' I turned to André. 'What do you think?'

'I think we're going to have a great time.'

The girls clapped their hands and hugged each other, a welcome change from the petty squabbling that so often marked the relationship between the thirteen-year-old Alice and her seven-year-old sister, Claudette.

The trip itself was uneventful. We spent Wednesday night at a motel on I-95 outside Fredericksburg, Virginia, and checked into the Marriott in downtown Greensboro at around 6 pm on Thursday.

We enjoyed a good sleep and a leisurely Friday morning before arriving just before noon at the auditorium of the University of North Carolina, Greensboro, as my alma mater was now known.

An usher guided the four of us through hundreds of people and scores of television cameras to reserved spots in the front row of the auditorium. The chancellor of UNC began proceedings, followed by speeches from a number of dignitaries—the only one I recognised was North Carolina Governor, Jim Hunt.

Four names were then called—Franklin McCain, David

Richmond, Ezell Blair and Joseph McNeil, who was resplendent in a US air force uniform with pilot's wings on his chest and the silver oak leaves of a lieutenant colonel on his shoulders.

The Greensboro Four ascended the stage where they received plaques honouring their civil rights activism. So far all according to plan.

Then came the surprise. I heard my name being called, along with that of Cynthia Partridge. I looked around and saw a frail, elderly woman being wheeled up to the stage in a wheelchair. What could I do? I followed suit.

Then Franklin McCain stepped to the podium.

'While David, Ezra, Joseph and I are very grateful for this honour, this event would not be complete if we didn't recognise the courage of two additional people, people who had no personal reason to involve themselves in our struggle for equal rights, but who did so, nonetheless. Despite the certainty of social ostracism, despite the very real risk of physical violence, these two brave women took a stand next to us that first day of the sit-in at Woolworths when they didn't have to. Ladies and gentlemen, I give you Mrs Cynthia Partridge and Mrs Josie Archambeau ... who I knew back in the day as Josie Stanton.'

The room erupted in loud applause and then Cynthia and I were presented with plaques, which I accepted like an automaton. To be honest, I was in a state of shock.

We were deluged by a mass of wellwishers and media who were seeking quotes and on-air interviews. I was only able to exchange a few brief words with Franklin, discovering that he had chosen a career in the chemical industry over medical school.

After shaking what seemed to be hundreds of hands and dodging journalists' questions, I signalled to André that I was done. It was time to slip away to our hotel. With a breath of relief, I left the auditorium with my family and we began to walk across campus towards the downtown Marriott.

When we arrived at the hotel we were ambushed by another pack of journalists and TV cameramen who were lying in wait in the lobby.

'No comment,' I repeated like a mantra as we pushed our way past to the elevators.

Back in our room at last, Alice turned to me with a quizzical expression. 'Mom, why don't you talk to the newspapers? You're a hero.'

I shook my head. 'I'm no hero, sweet girl. At least I don't feel like one.'

'Well, I think you are,' declared Alice. 'And so do all those other people who gave you that plaque.'

'So do I,' echoed Claudette, who picked up the plaque from where it lay on the bed and began to read aloud. 'In recognition of Mrs Josephine Archambeau for ...'

'That's enough,' I interrupted, as I reclaimed the plaque, packing it away in my suitcase.

'Your mom is modest, sweetheart,' André explained.

'I know that, papa,' replied Alice. 'But I still think she deserves to be honoured.'

'Well, now she is honoured, no?'

'I suppose,' sighed Alice.

'Come here, girls,' I said, patting the bed to indicate they should sit down beside me.

'I did a very small thing a long time ago,' I explained, 'but it was nothing like the actions of people like Martin Luther King, Jr, or Rosa Parks. They're the real heroes of the civil rights struggle.

I don't want to distract from those who deserve to be honoured. Do you understand?'

Alice pondered this and then nodded. 'I get it, Mom. I don't like it, but I get it.'

'Good,' I replied, enveloping my two daughters in a hug. I turned to André. 'How about we leave early?'

His eyebrows rose. 'As in now?'

I nodded. 'I want to go home.'

'All right, girls,' announced André. 'Pack up your things. We'll be leaving in a few minutes.'

'I'll drive,' I said as we entered the parking lot after checking out of the hotel. A few minutes' drive brought us to the on-ramp of the I–40 leading east to Durham. The Greensboro skyline soon receded in our rear-view mirror, and with it my five minutes of fame.

Obscurity suited me. Let others seek the limelight. For my part, I was happy to disappear into the shadows of normal life and focus on those thousand little things that, in the aggregate, help to make the world better.

4. THE MARCH ON WASHINGTON

28 August 1963

By the time I strode through the south-east entrance to the Old Senate Office Building, Constitution Avenue was already packed with people, mostly African American, but with a smattering of white faces among the crowd as well. They were all moving in a massive but orderly procession towards the Lincoln Memorial some two and a half miles away at the western end of the National Mall.

That day, Wednesday 28 August 1963, was a normal workday, but I wheedled permission from my chief of staff to attend the March on Washington. My sales pitch was that the event would be a great opportunity to collect colourful details and anecdotes for use in the senator's speeches. After only a few months in the United States Senate, Abe Ribicoff had already established a name for himself as one of that body's most ardent supporters of civil rights, a cause I felt privileged to support through my modest talents as his wordsmith and speechwriter.

Descending the granite steps onto Constitution Avenue, I slipped into the throng, finding myself surrounded by people in their Sunday best. Many of the women wore colourful dresses and, in some cases, cotton gloves, while the men were clad in suits, ties and hats. I inferred that this dress code was an unspoken expression of respect for the man we were all marching to hear—the Reverend Martin Luther King, Jr.

The weather was unseasonably pleasant for a city notorious for its searing summers. Yet while the ambient Washington DC temperature was only 75 degrees, the mass of bodies produced their own heat, raising the temperature still higher. But perspiration was a small price to pay for the chance to participate in such a landmark occasion, at least, that's how I felt at the time. Later, for reasons that will become clear, I would have cause for concern about the niceties of personal hygiene.

We made our way down Constitution Avenue without impediment, the police having blocked off every intersecting street running north–south. The officers I saw were clad not only in the familiar light blue of the DC metro police, but in a hodgepodge of uniforms that signalled affiliation with various law enforcement agencies around Washington. There were officers from Montgomery and Prince George counties in Maryland and Fairfax County in Virginia, and from the nearby cities of Arlington and Alexandria as well.

I read in the next day's *Washington Post* that the number of police mobilised for this event totalled over four thousand. All for naught. The constabulary was left largely unemployed by the impeccable public order maintained by the crowd throughout the march.

We were crossing 15th Street NW, with the White House Ellipse ahead on our right and the Washington Monument on our left, when a lovely soprano voice broke out into a beautiful rendition of 'We Shall Overcome'. I'm not ashamed to admit that there was a tear in my eye as I joined others in the refrain of that soulful civil rights anthem.

By 17th Street NW, it was clear there was no way I would get anywhere near the Lincoln Memorial. I angled my way around the Main Navy Building and encountered a mammoth crowd spilling across the paths and grass on either side of the reflecting pool. A veritable thicket of protest signs loomed above the heads of the crowd, some calling for civil rights, others for equitable pay or fair access to housing.

I managed to thread my way to within five hundred yards of the Lincoln Memorial before the crowd prevented me from getting any closer approach. I had just claimed a patch of vacant lawn when the first strains of the 'Star-spangled Banner' brought me—and everyone in the crowd to our feet. The national anthem was followed by an invocation by a Catholic priest, who I later learned was the Archbishop of Washington.

I settled back down, and a series of speakers ascended to the podium, one after the other. Some of these orators would become quite famous in their own right, future congressman John Lewis, for one. But, quite frankly, I was more interested in the cute girl who was walking by, looking for a place to sit.

'Please join me,' I offered, making space on the grass while flashing, what I hoped was, my most dazzling smile.

She reciprocated with a smile of her own, which revealed flawless teeth. 'Thank you. I'm Rosslyn Seamons.'

'Anthony Milo,' I replied, extending my hand.

She accepted my greeting with a smile that set my heart pounding.

'So, what's brought you to the march?' she asked.

'I'm working for Senator Abe Ribicoff,' I said, 'so I have a professional and personal reason for being here.'

'Personal?' she said.

'You don't have to be black to recognise injustice,' I said, trying not to sound too pompous.

She smiled and nodded, and we fell silent for a time.

As the parade of warm-up speakers continued at the podium, I kept glancing at her out of the corner of my eye. I couldn't stop. She was gorgeous—coffee-coloured complexion, almond-coloured eyes, shoulder-length black hair, a slender frame—I was entranced.

I mustered up the courage to continue the conversation. 'So, Rosslyn Seamons, what do you do when you're not on Washington?'

'I'm a senior at Barnard,' she replied, with another lovely smile.

'So, you're from New York?' I asked.

Rosslyn shook her head. 'Wilmington.'

'I'm an upstater,' I replied. 'Albany born and bred. My dad runs the Appeals Division of the New York Solicitor General's office.'

'Nice. And what about his son?' she asked.

'Graduated from Princeton last year and now I write speeches for Senator Ribicoff. I also help the press secretary with media.'

'Wow, I'm impressed,' said Rosslyn, bowing her head in a purse-lipped nod of respect. 'So, what's the master plan? Law school like Daddy?'

'What makes you think there is a master plan?'

'Don't you preppy Ivy League types always have one?' she challenged with a grin.

I shrugged. 'Don't know. Maybe the Peace Corps, but I'm having fun on the Hill, so I'll stay in DC for a while. And you?'

'I'm an English major, so I'm hoping for a gig with one of the big publishers in New York.'

'I was an English major too,' I grinned.

As the conversation turned to our favourite works of

literature—Webster's *Duchess of Malfi* for me and Brontë's *Wuthering Heights* for her—we were oblivious to the orators taking their turn at the dais. Engrossed in one another, we paid little heed to people we'd never heard of and in whom we had little interest, until a pure contralto voice issued from the loudspeakers singing a spiritual hymn I had never heard before.

'That's Mahalia Jackson,' gasped Rosslyn, her lips almost touching my ear. A world-famous singer may have been performing her magic, but I was far more entranced by the proximity of this fascinating girl.

After Mahalia, it was the turn of a man wearing a yarmulke—presumably a rabbi—to speak.

'Will you have dinner with me?' I said, oblivious to the rabbinical words of wisdom echoing from the speakers.

'Aren't you getting a bit ahead of yourself?' she asked, her rhetorical question accompanied by a smile. 'We just met.'

'The heart wants what it wants,' I replied.

'Dickinson,' replied Rosslyn with a nod of approval.

'So?' I pressed. 'Will you? Have dinner with me?'

She smiled and opened her mouth to respond just as the speakers reverberated with that unique sing-song oratorical cadence that was the trademark of Dr Martin Luther King, Jr.

A hush fell over the mall as people hung on every word—including Rosslyn and me. There's little need for me to quote the text of a speech that has entered the annals of history as one of the greatest ever delivered. I'm sure that you, my readers, are familiar with Dr King's call to honour the national promissory note that was yet uncashed for America's black population. I am confident you've all read or heard his reference, expressed at the urging of famed blues singer Mahalia Jackson, to the dream that his children will one day be judged by character rather than skin colour.

By the end of the speech—some seventeen minutes later—Rosslyn and I were both in tears, tears because the emotive impact of the Dr King's message was irresistible to anyone with a functional moral compass. As I reached over to intertwine my fingers with hers, I felt awe as well, awe because as a novice political speechwriter I found myself in the presence of greatness. While I might emulate and aspire to the eloquence of Dr King, there was no way my words would achieve the impact of what I had just witnessed. And I was perfectly fine with that.

After closing remarks by someone named A Philip Randolph—one of the march organisers, I later learned—the crowd began to disperse in the same quiet, orderly manner in which it had assembled.

'So, what about that dinner?' I asked while helping Rosslyn to her feet.

She looked up with eyes still wet with tears, which didn't detract a single iota from her beauty, at least in my view.

'I don't know,' she mused, as we began to walk eastwards along the mall.

'What don't you know?'

Rosslyn looked up at me with a sombre expression. 'I'm a serious girl and you're Italian.'

'I don't understand.'

'I'm not ... easy,' she said with a slight edge of defiance.

'Whoa!' I protested, raising my hands. 'If I've done anything ...'

'No, no,' she replied with a decisive shake of the head. 'You've been lovely, a perfect gentleman, but you still are who you are.'

'Meaning what?'

'Meaning if we continue this ... friendship, at some point I'll have to meet your family. They'll be expecting you to bring home an Italian girl named Raffaella, not a black girl named Rosslyn.'

I laughed. 'My parents will be fine ... I think. And, if not, it'll be World War III.'

Rosslyn glanced at me with a quizzical frown. 'You know, you're nuts. You've only known me a couple of hours.'

'Who ever loved that loved not at first sight?'

She laughed. 'As an English major you're surely aware that *As You Like It* is a comedy.'

I gently put my hands on her shoulders. 'The Bard may have been joking, but I'm serious.'

I leaned down and delivered a soft kiss to her lips. She didn't recoil or pull away—a good sign.

'Now, about that dinner,' I said. 'What sort of food do you like?'

Rosslyn smiled. 'You know Ben's Chili Bowl?'

I shook my head.

'I guess U Street is off the beaten track for Hill types like yourself,' she laughed. 'But it has the best chilli dogs and milkshakes in Washington.'

'Deal,' I replied. 'We can either catch the bus, or walk to my place and take my car.'

'And where's your place?' she asked.

'Dupont Circle.'

Rosslyn gazed at me in silent appraisal before nodding. 'Okay, then an early dinner before I catch the train back to New York.'

I smiled. 'Great. After we eat, I'll take you to Union Station. Hopefully, the mad rush of people leaving town will be over by then and the train won't be crowded.'

I led the way through the gap between the Munitions Building and Main Navy Building across Constitution Avenue into 20th Street NW, past the Federal Reserve. Twentieth was one of the smaller streets leading into Foggy Bottom, taking us off the beaten path of the masses who were leaving the Lincoln Memorial area.

As we walked, we talked, about family first—I had an older sister while she grew up as a 'sandwich' kid between two brothers; about religion—I was a lapsed Catholic while she was a believing Baptist; about what we wanted from life—I supposed I'd end up following Dad's footsteps into the law, while she had her sights set on becoming a literary agent.

With each exchange, I felt the conversation becoming easier and easier, like nothing I had ever experienced before. It was ... comfortable, as if I'd finally come home after a long journey.

*

The story of how Rosslyn and I met at the March on Washington became a staple of family lore. Our relationship flourished after I dropped her off that night at Union Station. We would see each other on most weekends, she making the four-hour trip from New York to DC one Friday, and I following suit in the opposite direction the next.

This back-and-forth continued for another year until September 1964 when I began law school at Columbia. That June she graduated from Barnard, moving into a junior editorial slot at Knopf. By this time, we'd each been introduced to each other's families. My parents and sisters fell in love with Rosslyn, and I got on well with her parents, who ran a mid-sized hardware store in the Quaker Hill neighbourhood of Wilmington, Delaware. There were a few discordant notes sounded by retrograde members of both our extended families, but all voices of familial dissent were stilled after our mothers read the riot act about respect for our relationship.

4. The March on Washington

As we were now both Manhattanites, Rosslyn and I were spending more nights together than apart. I suppose it was fair to say that we were pretty much living together. My parents were fine with that arrangement, while Rosslyn's devoutly Baptist mother and father affected ignorance of our pre-marital cohabitation.

At the end of my first year of law school, I felt it was time to take things up a notch. I booked a table at Tavern on the Green in Central Park, ostensibly to celebrate the fact that my good grades had won me a coveted spot on the student-edited *Columbia Law Review*. A stint as a law review editor was seen as a golden ticket to post–law school employment.

However, I had a hidden agenda. I had something else on my mind—nothing too elaborate, no marching bands nor drifts of balloons. Between the main course and dessert, I simply rose from my chair and went down on one knee. Pulling a month's salary worth of diamond ring from my pocket, I asked her to marry me. This was two years before the 1967 *Loving v Virginia* Supreme Court ruling that found Jim Crow miscegenation laws to be unconstitutional—but we were in New York City, not New Orleans.

She, of course, said yes, and the rest is history. And, speaking of history, after my retirement from a career as a litigator and judge, I decided to spend time on a personal account of the march. For several months I ensconced myself at the New York Public Library, where I researched the clash of egos and agendas that lay behind the organisation of the event.

The prime movers behind the march were union leader A Philip Randolph and civil rights activist Bayard Rustin. By early 1963, those two activists had recruited an organising committee that began putting the pieces in place for a protest march to be conducted in August in Washington DC. Headlining the event would be Dr Martin Luther King, Jr, of the Southern Christian Leadership Conference. He would be joined by James Farmer of the Congress of Racial Equality and John Lewis of the Student Non-Violent Coordinating Committee. Also included were Roy Wilkins of the NAACP and Whitney Young of the National Urban League—and, of course, A Philip Randolph. This committee, excluding Bayard Rustin, soon became known as the Big Six.

Some of the Big Six organisers objected to the involvement of Bayard Rustin in the march on account of his open homosexuality and former brief membership of the Young Communist League. This issue was brought to a head by segregationist South Carolina Senator Strom Thurmond, who introduced the record of Rustin's sodomy arrest into the Congressional Record, having been alerted to it by J Edgar Hoover. Yet despite this negative publicity, A Philip Randolph insisted that Rustin be included in the organising effort. The other members of the Big Six grudgingly agreed that Rustin should be allowed to play a behind-the-scenes role in the march, which by that stage was to be held in two weeks.

In June 1963, the Big Six had invited four white leaders to join the organising effort for the march, producing what henceforth became known as the 'Big Ten'. These new additions included Walter Reuther of the United Auto Workers (UAW); the Reverend Eugene Carson Blake representing the Protestant National Council of Churches; Mathew Ahmann of the National Catholic Conference for Interracial Justice; and Rabbi Joachim Prinz of the American Jewish Congress.

This broadening of the tent led to disagreements over strategy among the Big Ten. The UAW's Reuther wanted the event to focus on economic equity, while the NAACP sought to emphasise the battle against Jim Crow segregation. At the end of the day, the final title of the march reflected a compromise between the economic focus of labour union activists and those who wished to highlight the struggle for civil rights.

Towards the end of June, the Big Ten had a dispiriting meeting with President John F Kennedy at the White House. Kennedy was less than enthusiastic about the prospect of a large-scale protest event in Washington, expressing concerns about reports that some activists were planning acts of civil disobedience. Only when organisers promised to forestall any breach of the peace did Kennedy bestow his political blessing in a statement made on 17 July.

Despite his relegation to a backroom role, Bayard Rustin was instrumental in organising the logistics for the march. He assembled a team of two hundred activists who generated publicity and coordinated transportation, which they hoped would bring large numbers of protesters to Washington. The mass turnout evident on the day of the march serves as testament to the success of Rustin and his team: the attendance of 200,000 people spoke for itself.

Yet, at the time, the prospect of a mass civil rights demonstration in the heartland of America's capital city was unsettling to much of the political establishment and not just to the diehard segregationists from the Jim Crow South.

FBI Director J Edgar Hoover was notorious for collecting incriminating evidence on anyone and everyone involved in American public life. He was resolutely opposed to the march, believing that the civil rights movement was part of a communist plot to destabilise the United States. Hoover angrily rejected reports from FBI investigators who found no evidence of Marxist infiltration among march organisers.

So, in the days leading up to 28 August, Hoover did what he

could to interfere and undermine the organising effort for the March on Washington. On his instructions, FBI agents contacted members of the Big Ten with lurid tales of communist influence, but J Edgar Hoover's Marxist conspiracy theories failed to dissuade any of the organisers from showing up on the day.

More nefarious was the indifference shown by the FBI towards the many threats of physical violence made against organisers of the march and media outlets that supported it. I decided then and there that the scandalous behaviour of J Edgar Hoover would rate an entire chapter in my book.

My research also brought to light other interesting snippets of information of which I had been unaware. I discovered that several dozen neo-Nazis had assembled in Washington to mount some sort of counter-protest against the march. I never saw any such thing because these swastika-wearing thugs were quickly swept up and arrested by police before trouble could be fomented.

I also found out, some forty years afterwards, that a slew of Hollywood celebrities attended the march. But, on the day, nobody paid much attention to them. It turned out that not even the Tinseltown lustre of Charlton Heston and Marlon Brando could outshine the brilliance of Dr Martin Luther King, Jr's oratory. Nevertheless, the roll-call was impressive. Actors who marched included Gregory Peck, Paul Newman, Sidney Poitier, Diahann Carroll, Burt Lancaster and James Garner. Singers and entertainers included Harry Belafonte, Judy Garland, Peter, Paul and Mary, Lena Horne, Joan Baez, Eartha Kitt, Bob Dylan, Josephine Baker, Marian Anderson and Sammy Davis, Jr; writer James Baldwin and director Joseph L Mankiewicz also marched. According to Garner, the FBI called each of them the night before with a warning not to march because their safety could not be guaranteed.

After a couple of years, I completed my manuscript, which I titled *March on the Mall: How 28 August 1963 changed my life and the life of America*. Pretentious, I know, which is probably a big part of the reason I couldn't find a publisher willing to take me on—this and the fact that lawyers are renowned for their stilted writing; all those 'aforementioneds' and seventy-word sentences filled with sub-clauses.

But none of that matters. I am content with the knowledge that future generations of Milos will be left an account of how their ancestors came together at one of the most momentous events of American history.

That is more than enough.

5. THE ASSASSINATION OF MALCOLM X

21 February 1965

Albert Camus wrote that every revolutionary ends up being either an oppressor or a heretic. When Malcolm X—born Malcolm Little—faced the choice between those two options, he chose the latter. And it killed him.

I know because I was there. Even worse, I was the man charged with his protection, and I failed.

In February 1965, I was one year out of the FBI academy and just over two months into an undercover assignment to infiltrate the Nation of Islam or NOI. My cover was that of an embittered former FBI special agent who'd been driven out by the racial bigotry of his superiors—a very plausible version of events in J Edgar Hoover's Federal Bureau of Investigation.

Our operational theory held that the NOI would jump at the chance to engage the services of a disaffected black, former FBI agent, who was a graduate of Cornell University. Yet the first feelers didn't come from the Nation itself, but from an aide to Malcolm X.

Like most things in life, the motivation for Malcolm's departure from the NOI in April 1964 was multifaceted and complex. It certainly generated considerable controversy. Some say the formal catalyst was Malcolm's discovery that NOI leader, Elijah Muhammad, was keeping an extramarital harem of young women. Others believe that Muhammad and other NOI leaders were jealous and resentful of Malcolm's prominent media presence. Regardless of the mix of factors that induced Malcolm X to leave NOI, one thing is clear; Elijah Muhammad didn't take kindly to the high-profile defection of his most charismatic lieutenant. Whether by design or spontaneous individual action, the assassination threats against him began almost immediately.

In May 1964, Malcolm X arrived home after participating in the Hajj pilgrimage to Mecca that was obligatory for all Muslims. He now saw himself as an orthodox Sunni Muslim and his exposure in Saudi Arabia to Islamic pilgrims of many nationalities caused him to rethink the doctrines of racial animosity that were central to NOI theology. Elijah Muhammad taught his followers that people of African descent were biologically superior to 'blue-eyed devils', his term for Caucasians. When Malcolm began to make public statements about the unity of all humanity, those who remained loyal to Nation of Islam were further enraged.

Two months later, in July 1964, Malcolm again departed on a tour of Africa, visiting almost a dozen nations and being feted by Egypt's Gamal Abdel Nasser, Ghana's Kwame Nkrumah and Algeria's Ahmed Ben Bella. He then travelled to France and the UK, where he participated in a debate at the Oxford Union over the proposition 'Extremism in defence of liberty is no vice'.

Malcolm returned to the US in early December 1964. A few days afterwards, I was invited to an interview at the Organization of Afro-American Unity headquarters—the OAAU—at the Hotel Theresa in Harlem. I entered the hotel without challenge or impediment and went directly to the door of Malcolm's suite on the sixteenth floor. I could have been carrying a bazooka.

I knocked and the door opened to reveal a heavy-set man who looked to be in his forties. I could see the bulge of a shoulder-holstered pistol beneath his left armpit.

'Rasheed,' he said by way of introduction.

'John Pearson,' I replied.

'Come in. He's waiting to meet you.'

'Thank you,' I said, concealing my feelings that the amateur-hour security regime had allowed me into Malcolm's presence without so much as a pat down for weapons.

I followed Rasheed into the sitting room of the suite, taking in the uncurtained floor-to-ceiling glass windows that would make the task of a sniper so much easier.

Malcolm rose from his seat and extended his hand in greeting. His slender build and six-feet-plus height gave him a prepossessing physical presence. I felt myself under keen observation by a fierce intelligence.

'Please sit down,' said Malcolm in that calm, cultured voice I had heard during numerous broadcast interviews. He examined the contents of a file that lay on the side table. 'Mr John Pearson. Tell me a bit about yourself.'

'Twenty-seven years old. Born in Decatur, Illinois. Graduate of Northwestern where I did Reserve Officers Training Corps. Four years in the army, mostly with the 7th ID in Korea. Then the FBI. But I presume you know all this already.'

I nodded towards the manila folder he held. John Pearson was my real name, as were the particulars of my biography, up to my fictitious resignation from the Bureau.

'Yes,' replied Malcolm with another glance at the file. 'Tell me more about your short period with the FBI. You appear to have done quite well as an army officer—platoon leader, assistant battalion operations officer. It says here they were prepared to offer you command of a rifle company if you signed on for another four years. So, what happened with the Feds?'

I shrugged. 'J Edgar Hoover is what happened. My platoon sergeant in Korea was named Christodoulopoulos. When we ran up against higher rank stupidity, he liked to quote an old Greek proverb about how the fish always stinks from the head. I graduated from the academy at Quantico without too many problems, but when I got to the Chicago field office, I encountered a collection of bigots starting with the special agent in charge. He set the tone for the entire office. I decided that I didn't want to spend the next forty years putting up with snide comments and racist jokes and no hope of promotion. So, I quit.'

Malcolm smiled. 'You thought you could bring about change from the inside?'

'I suppose so,' I replied, with another shrug.

Malcolm sighed. 'The only way we will ever be able to change the prejudiced structure of America is through unrelenting political pressure.'

'No argument here.'

'So why me?' asked Malcolm. 'Why do you want to put your life at risk to be my bodyguard?'

'Simple. You left the Nation. While I understand why Elijah Muhammad's angry, I can't condone his bigotry. When he says that whites are racially inferior to blacks, he becomes the mirror image of the Klan. I think we're better than that, and I think you provide the sort of moral leadership black America needs right now.'

'Are you a Muslim?' asked Malcolm.

'I grew up Baptist,' I replied. 'But now? Let's just say I'm in a questioning phase.'

Malcolm perused me for a moment before turning to address Rasheed. 'What do you think?'

Rasheed shrugged. 'His background checks out. And Allah knows we could do with a professional in these matters.'

Malcolm nodded and turned back to me. 'Speaking of expertise, what do you make of our security arrangements?'

I paused. 'Are you looking for an honest answer?'

'That's precisely what I'm looking for,' Malcolm replied. 'Don't worry about offending Rasheed. He was an accountant before all this. He won't mind a forthright analysis.'

'Amateur hour,' I said. 'There is no external security on the building. I wasn't challenged, much less searched, as I made my way to your suite. And Rasheed let me in without patting me down for weapons.'

'Well ... that's because you were expected,' Rasheed replied in a tone of embarrassed apology.

'Rule number one, always expect the unexpected,' I declared. 'No one outside Malcolm's family and vetted advisers gets close without being checked for weapons.'

Malcolm smiled and glanced again at Rasheed who nodded in response.

'Very well, John. It'll be up to you to tighten things up. How does $10,000 per annum sound?'

I paused, blinking in surprise. He was offering me a sum that was slightly more than my salary as an FBI special agent. 'Very generous, thanks.'

Malcolm nodded. 'Your title will be deputy chief of security.

We don't want to create the perception that Rasheed's work has been found wanting, but, in reality, you'll be running the show.'

I glanced at Rasheed, who responded with a smiling nod.

'Welcome to the team,' said Malcolm.

'Thank you very much,' I replied, shaking his outstretched hand.

'I'd like you to begin immediately. I'll be travelling overseas in early February, so between now and my departure I hope you'll be able to implement improvements to our security arrangements as you see fit.'

I nodded. 'That shouldn't be a problem. I need background information on the members of the security team. Military experience, if any. Weapons training. That sort of thing. And do I have authorisation to recruit if the existing complement is unsatisfactory?'

'Subject to our approval,' replied Rasheed.

I nodded, thinking that this might be a good opportunity to bring in someone else from the Bureau or NYPD undercover. 'Will you be needing me to accompany you on that overseas trip?'

Malcolm shook his head. 'I don't think there'll be a need. The last time I was in England I had close protection from Scotland Yard. You should focus your efforts on reorganising our security here at home while I'm away.'

'Very well,' I replied. 'I'll see you tomorrow then.'

I left the Hotel Theresa, going home to my apartment in Brooklyn Heights where I phoned my handler at the FBI field office in Manhattan.

He was a six-foot-two, former college linebacker named McDougal who was overjoyed at the news of my new job. I inferred from his rapturous reaction that the FBI brass made no distinction between Malcolm and Elijah Muhammad. J Edgar didn't care that Malcolm had abandoned Muhammad's teachings of hatred towards non-blacks. There was no room for nuance in the view of the US government. These people were all lumped together in the singular category of disloyal black nationalists who were a threat to public safety. In fact, because of his charisma, his eloquence and his ability to inspire, Malcolm was viewed as a greater threat by J Edgar Hoover. I later learned that the attitude of the FBI led to far worse abuses of power, but more about that later.

At the time, I felt I had a job to do and put my qualms aside for another day. My job was to guarantee the safety of a man I was beginning to respect. It didn't matter that my superiors didn't share my growing faith in the character of Malcolm X. I rationalised that there was no contradiction between my cover role and my real job.

The next day I arrived at the Hotel Theresa at 9 am sharp and got to work. The backgrounds of the four men who constituted Malcolm's security team were disappointing, to say the least. No time in the military, even as rear echelon clerks, much less infantrymen. I resolved to take training into my own hands. Anonymous threats of death and mayhem were arriving fast and furiously. The FBI file was bulging with intelligence from confidential informants and wiretaps about ongoing assassination plots. One telephone transcript dated 8 June 1964 showed Malcolm's wife, Betty, receiving threats from an unknown caller that her husband was as good as dead.

I decided we would start the new security regime at the range, where I could gauge the proficiency of my fellow bodyguards with the basics of personal security. The following weekend I convinced Malcolm to cancel all public appearances, while I took the not-so-fearsome foursome out to the Catskills for a day of firearms skills assessment. The first order of business was replacing the .38 revolvers they carried with something more effective. The Colt M1911 semi-automatic pistol, which I carried during my time as an infantry officer in Korea, was a much better choice. Its 0.45 calibre round was much more likely to put a target down.

In addition to my personal M1911, I was able to secure two other pistols and four hundred rounds of ammunition. We began with dry fire drills and progressed to live ammo. These were no Wyatt Earps, but by the end of the day I felt that at least they knew which end of the weapon to point at an assailant.

My basic training regime continued, and by mid-January 1965, I was beginning to be reasonably satisfied with the new security arrangements. The desk staff at Hotel Theresa had standing orders to notify us of any visitors and I always had one man on duty in the corridor outside our suite. Another man routinely spent the night on the couch in Malcolm's living room when he was home.

My primary source of concern arose from his frequent public speeches and appearances before crowds numbering in the scores, if not the hundreds. Such events were, by definition, difficult to secure without the manpower and resources of, say, the Secret Service.

Meanwhile, I dutifully reported to McDougal, describing my activities as a means of solidifying my cover. I neglected to let my FBI handler know of my affection and respect for Malcolm lest I be accused of 'going native'. In a manner of speaking, I suppose that's precisely what happened.

I was quite relieved when I left Malcolm at the gate of his Pan Am flight from JFK to Heathrow on 5 February 1965. With him an ocean away from potential NOI assassins, I could breathe freely and continue my efforts to tighten the security envelope around him. But the respite from worry was brief. I picked Malcolm up at JFK on his return from Britain on 13 February.

Since his defection, the NOI had taken legal action to force Malcolm from his home in the East Elmhurst neighbourhood of Queens where he lived with wife Betty and their four daughters. There was a judicial expulsion order pending, but Malcolm's lawyers filed for a stay order and appeal. Just after 2 am on the morning of 15 February 1965, someone decided that the court process was just too cumbersome. A Molotov cocktail was thrown through the home's front window into the living room, forcing Malcolm and his family to flee in their nightclothes into the street.

I was not on duty that night, and arrived thirty minutes later to find the brick-and-shingle home ablaze, with smoke and cinders billowing into the night sky. Malcolm sat on the opposite sidewalk trying to comfort his newly pregnant wife and children as firefighters battled to contain the blaze. We later found out that a second Molotov cocktail had been thrown at the rear of the house, but had failed to ignite.

My immediate response was to hustle Malcolm, Betty and the girls into my car. It was a squeeze, but moving them to safety was my immediate priority. After secreting his wife and children at a safe house that I had secured for just such a contingency, I took Malcolm aside.

'This changes everything,' I told him.

Malcolm shook his head. 'I don't see how. I've had death threats before.'

'Malcolm, there are threats and there is action. Your home was just firebombed. You have to cancel your public appearances until we get the security situation sorted. At least wait until I talk to the police.'

'The police?' snorted Malcolm. 'Don't be naïve. The NYPD and your precious FBI would be happy to see me dead in a ditch. We must look to our own devices. Besides, we're beginning to work up some political momentum. I can't stop now.'

I threw up my hands ... literally ... and continued to do the best I could in the circumstances. On 19 February, I escorted Malcolm to an interview with documentary filmmaker Gordon Parks. In the middle of the interview Malcolm declared in the most casual of tones that the Nation of Islam was trying to kill him. Parks started in surprise while a shiver ran down my spine. I can't honestly say that I had a premonition that Malcolm's words would come true just a few days later, but I walked away from that interview with knots in my stomach.

The next event on Malcolm's calendar was a meeting of the Organization of Afro-American Unity, or OAAU, at the Audubon Ballroom at Broadway and 165th Street in Washington Heights near the northern tip of Manhattan. The OAAU was a group founded by Malcolm after his departure from the NOI. Secular in orientation, the objective of the OAAU was to unite American blacks across the religious spectrum in a campaign for civil rights that would take a more militant tone.

The Audubon event was going to be a big deal, with several hundred people expected to attend what we hoped would be regarded as a landmark speech. With a security detail numbering only four, the task of searching every incoming member of the audience for weapons would be difficult and time-consuming. On Saturday, the day before his speech, Malcolm told me that he wanted to forego body searches at the Audubon.

'Sorry, but that's just nuts,' I snorted, making no attempt to hide my frustration and dismay.

Malcolm placed a calming hand on my shoulder. 'Brother John, building broad-based support for the OAAU is our top priority right now. We can't afford to alienate potential supporters by making people wait in line while we pat them down.'

I grimaced. 'It won't do the OAAU any good if you end up dead.'

Malcolm smiled. 'It's all in Allah's hands, my brother. I trust you will do your best to protect us, and that will have to be enough.'

I sighed in reluctant resignation and took my leave.

It was consistent with my cover as Malcolm's assistant chief of security to contact the NYPD for assistance. It wasn't that I was naïve, but after dealing with the utter indifference of detectives charged with investigating the firebombing of Malcolm's home in Queens, I had few expectations. I telephoned the 33rd Precinct all the same.

'Thank you very much for your concern,' replied the detective with whom I spoke, 'We'll give the matter all due consideration.'

'Due consideration my ass,' I spat into the telephone before hanging up. I broke protocol by contacting my FBI handler from a pay phone, something that was only supposed to happen if I felt my life was in imminent danger. Needless to say, McDougal was less than thrilled to hear that my security concerns involved Malcolm rather than myself. He promised to pass my message up the chain to the assistant director in charge of the New York field office. However, his tone of voice left me less than confident that there would be any help forthcoming from that quarter.

That Sunday 21 February 1965, I arrived at the Audubon at 1.30 pm, half an hour before Malcolm was scheduled to begin his address. Climbing the stairs to the second-floor ballroom, I saw a lectern positioned at the head of a room filled with rows of folding chairs.

Malcolm arrived shortly with his wife and children, escorted by Rasheed and the other four members of the security detail. Malcolm cast an affectionate smile towards Betty Shabazz as she guided their daughters to reserved seats in the front row. The Audubon speech was going to be an all-hands-on-deck affair.

The local minister who was supposed to emcee the event failed to show, much to Malcolm's displeasure. So, at around 2.20 pm, one of Malcolm's personal assistants, a young man who went by the name of Benjamin 2x Goodman, strode to the podium.

'Good afternoon, ladies and gentlemen,' Goodman announced. 'Without further ado, it is my honour now to introduce a man who would give his life for his people.'

I remember thinking that Goodman's introduction was in rather poor taste as Malcolm strode forward, placing a small pile of cue cards on the podium. In accordance with my training, I, and another security team member, assumed our places on either flank; Malcolm had stipulated that no more than two of us should be visible to the audience for fear of alienating the very people he hoped to win over to his cause.

Malcolm had barely uttered 'As-Salaam Alaikum', when the crowd's murmured response was interrupted by sounds of a scuffle erupting from the fourth row of seats.

'Get your hand outta my pocket,' screamed a dark-skinned man.

As I, and everyone else in the security team, moved to quell this disturbance, I saw another black man out of the corner of my eye. He was lighting a match to what appeared to be a strip of photographic film. The film protruded like a fuse from what looked like a sock filled with something. Once the film was alight, the man threw the object towards the front of the room, where it fizzled and began to emit foul-smelling clouds of grey smoke.

In the meantime, Malcolm stepped around the lectern, his palms raised in a gesture of peace. 'Now brothers, break it up. Hold it, hold it.'

That's when it happened. A man, also sitting in the fourth row, pulled a sawn-off shotgun from beneath his coat and fired almost point blank into Malcolm's torso.

Watching Betty Shabazz trying to cover her daughters with her own body, I acted out of instinct to help move them out of harm's way.

Behind my back, I heard more gunshots and turned to see two other men charging towards Malcolm's prone body firing pistols as they ran. To my everlasting chagrin, I never even drew my own weapon, much less fired a single round in response.

The room erupted in panic, and in the confusion most of the assassins were able to escape. By then I was concerned with getting Malcolm to the ER at Columbia Presbyterian Hospital, which was literally just across the street and arranging for the evacuation of Betty Shabazz and the children after she'd followed his stretcher, weeping, across the street.

But all attempts to save him were to no avail. After taking a load of buckshot to the chest and with six more pistol bullets lodged in his body, Malcolm stood no chance. He was declared dead at 3.30 pm.

Looking across the street from the hospital, I could see that the Audubon Ballroom was now flooded by uniformed and plainclothes NYPD officers.

'Too little, too late,' I muttered. Sick at heart, I left the hospital and made my way back to my own apartment in Greenwich Village. With Malcolm gone, I could see no purpose in continuing my undercover assignment. Besides, I had some serious thinking to do.

The next morning, I walked into the FBI New York field office in violation of every rule the Bureau had ever developed to govern the behaviour of undercover operations. My fellow special agents looked at me in shock as I strode through the rows of desks to the door of the assistant director in charge, affectionately known as the ADiC.

Pushing past the protests of his secretary, I entered without knocking, interrupting an ongoing meeting between the ADiC and three people I didn't recognise.

'Did you get my message?' I challenged, my tone insubordinate. I didn't care.

The ADiC glanced up at me with the aplomb of a practiced diplomat before turning to the other participants in his meeting.

'Why don't we take a break? Twenty minutes?'

Recognising their cue, the three suits left the office.

'Special Agent Pearson, you seem to be in breach of protocol.'

'I only have one question,' I barked. 'Did McDougal pass along my warning about the danger of an assassination attempt against Malcolm X?'

The ADiC said nothing for several moments while perusing me carefully. 'You appear to have confused your priorities, special agent. Malcolm X was the target of an undercover investigation in which you played a laudable role, a role that will generate promising opportunities for your future in the Bureau.'

'Thank you for that, sir,' I replied, struggling to produce a conciliatory tone. 'But I saw this assassination coming. Malcolm's home was firebombed last week. I asked for help from both the Bureau and the NYPD and nothing was forthcoming.'

The ADiC pursed his lips. 'Special Agent McDougal did indeed pass on your request. But the Bureau isn't in the business of providing personal protection to … dangerous radicals.'

I nodded in grim comprehension. Reaching into my pocket, I took out my FBI shield and ID and laid them on the ADiC's desk.

'Are you sure about this, Special Agent Pearson?'

There was nothing left for me to say. I rose to my feet, turned on my heel and walked out of the FBI New York field office without a word.

Only years later I discovered that my undercover operation

was part of a much larger FBI dirty-tricks campaign designed to foment distrust and disunity among African American civil rights organisations. Code-named 'COINTELPRO', the program used tactics and surveillance, and outright forgery to undermine the credibility of progressive groups that were labelled subversive by the US government.

The existence of COINTELPRO was leaked to the media in 1971, causing J Edgar Hoover to cancel the program a year later, supposedly. But in view of the fact that G Gordon Liddy of Watergate break-in infamy was heavily involved in COINTELPRO, it's reasonable to assume that Hoover's cancellation was in name only.

In any event, the full sordid details of this domestic spying program were only revealed in 1976, by a US Senate investigation into intelligence community abuses led by Senator Frank Church. I was shocked to learn that some COINTELPRO operations were authorised by Robert F Kennedy, who was serving as his brother JFK's attorney-general. Another of my heroes turned out to have feet of authoritarian clay.

By this time, I was a practising paediatrician in Greenville, South Carolina, having in the interim gone to medical school after my resignation from the FBI.

Why medicine? After being played for a pawn by the US government, I sought out a profession that would enable me to earn a good living while giving back to the community, all without the taint of politics. I had ruled out my other prospective option—a career in the law.

And South Carolina? Well, growing up in Chicago with its brutal lake-effect snow, I was looking for a more congenial climate. I found it in Greenville, a lovely town in the Piedmont region noted for its mild winters and moderate summers.

I wanted to work in the South for other reasons as well. Even though the Civil Rights and Voting Rights Acts had been passed in 1964 and 1965 respectively, the African American community in former Jim Crow states still suffered the residual effects of slavery and second-class citizenship. When I qualified as a physician in 1972, poverty rates among black South Carolinians were among the worst in America. I thought that devoting one day per week to pro bono community clinic work would be a fitting response to that need.

In retrospect, I realise that I allowed myself to be a tool by becoming an unwitting participant in a domestic espionage program that targeted a great man, a man who was working for the betterment of my own community. This folly is my ongoing private shame.

I have never shared this chapter of my life with anyone other than my wife and life partner, Gayle, and I have no way of knowing whether this memoir will be of interest to anyone. Nonetheless, I feel compelled to set my story down.

To anyone reading these words, I express two hopes—one, that you find my story to be at least of modest interest, and two, that you can find it in your heart to forgive that young man who allowed himself to be taken down a wrong path.

END NOTE

In recent years there has been growing speculation as to whether the US government's role in the assassination of Malcolm X might be more sin of commission than omission. The hypothesis of direct government involvement was floated in a six-part documentary series screened on Netflix in early 2020.

Titled *Who Killed Malcolm X*, the documentary argued that the two men convicted of the crime, Thomas Johnson (aka Khalil Islam) and Norman 3X Butler (aka Muhammad Abdul Aziz) were not even present at the Audubon Ballroom that day. A NYPD detective assigned to the case admitted many years later that the investigation was botched.

The documentary demonstrated conclusively that the assassination was conducted by four members of an NOI mosque in Newark, New Jersey. More sinister was the hypothesis that official indifference to the likely murder of Malcolm X was a deliberate strategy by the government.

Benjamin Franklin famously quipped that the only way for three men to keep a secret is if two of them are dead. It is more than likely that COINTELPRO wiretaps and other forms of surveillance would have uncovered the plot to kill Malcolm before it was executed.

The 1960s were a time of tremendous upheaval and social turbulence in the US. The civil rights movement and opposition to the war in Vietnam were stirring up American society. The powers that be were terrified of communal strife and radical subversion.

We know that the FBI was conducting close surveillance on Martin Luther King, Jr, whom J Edgar Hoover regarded as a dangerous communist agent. Is it so far-fetched to consider that the US government might turn a blind eye to the elimination of Malcolm X, a man equally eloquent but far more radical than Martin Luther King, Jr?

It is likely that definitive evidence to answer this question will remain buried in US government archives for decades, if not centuries, to come.

6. SELMA TO MONTGOMERY MARCH

6 March 1965

Morris swallowed and squared his shoulders before inserting his key into the front door and opening it. 'Ma?'

He heard the sharp clatter of heels on wooden flooring as Mrs Anne Glazen walked down the entry hall.

'Morrie!' she exclaimed, holding out her arms as she rushed to embrace him. 'It's the middle of the semester. What are you doing here?'

'I took leave of absence, Ma. A group of us are going down to Alabama for the civil rights march.'

'But this is your last year,' Mrs Glazen protested, her hand covering her heart. 'You're about to graduate in a couple of months. You've been accepted to Columbia for law school! Have you forgotten?'

'I know, Ma. But this is too important. I have to be a part of it. I have to make a statement.'

'What are you talking about, Morrie?'

'There's going to be a civil rights march from Selma to Montgomery in Alabama. They say Martin Luther King, Jr, will be leading it, or maybe John Lewis.'

'I don't like the sound of this,' said Mrs Glazen 'Those whites in the South act like Cossacks. They murdered those two Jewish boys last year. Goodman and ...'

'Schwerner,' sighed Morris, 'Michael Schwerner. There was a black guy killed as well, Ma. James Chaney—and that's the whole point. Doesn't Rabbi Jacobson tell us, "*Tzedek, tzedek tir'dof*? Justice, justice thou shalt pursue?" What could be more just than ending Jim Crow in America?'

'But Morrie, they passed that law in Congress last year.'

'The Civil Rights Act? Yeah, Ma, but negroes still face serious discrimination when they try to register for the vote.'

'I know it's bad,' said Mrs Glazen, 'but why do you have to go? You have your whole life ahead of you.'

Morris approached his mother and placed a gentle hand on either shoulder. 'Remember what Rabbi Hillel says in the Talmud, Ma. "If I am not for myself, who is for me? But if I am only for myself, what am I? And if not now, when?" I have to go. I have to take a stand. Those are the values you taught me.'

Anne Glazen put her head on her eldest son's chest. 'It's just that I see what is happening on the TV news. I'll worry about you.'

'I'll be fine, Ma,' said Morris, patting her on the back. 'I won't be alone. People are coming from all over the country. We'll have strength in numbers.'

Mrs Glazen pulled away and set off down the hall. 'Well, you should eat something, Mister Strength-in-numbers. Come into the kitchen and I'll fix you a sandwich,' she said over her shoulder.

Morris trailed his mother into the kitchen. 'No time. I just came home to get my camera. There are people coming by to pick me up.'

Mrs Glazen looked up from the loaf of bread she'd taken out.

'Can't you at least wait until Simon and Hannah get home from school?'

Morris shook his head. 'Like I said, my ride will be here any minute.'

His mother sighed. 'Then go and get what you need. By the time you're done I'll have your sandwich ready.'

Morris bounded up the stairs to his bedroom and rummaged through the closet until he found his Canonflex RM and eight rolls of unused film.

Making his way downstairs, he heard three short honks from the street.

'Ma, they're here.'

Morris slipped his camera and film into his knapsack, placing it in the middle between layers of folded clothing.

Mrs Glazen rushed into the hallway, a paper bag in her outstretched hand.

'How many friends do you have?'

'Three.'

'Good,' said Mrs Glazen. 'I made four corned-beef sandwiches with relish and mustard.'

Morris dropped a kiss on his mother's cheek, shouldered his knapsack and left through the front door. His mother followed.

'Be careful!' she admonished from the front step.

Morris waved as he clambered into the back seat of the turquoise-blue Ford Mustang convertible parked in front of his house.

'I have food,' he announced, distributing the sandwiches to the other occupants of the Mustang, a blue-eyed blonde at the wheel and a brunette in the front passenger seat.

'Goodbye, Mrs Glazen,' shouted the blonde with a friendly wave. 'Thank you for the sandwiches!'

Elizabeth Willoughby put the Mustang into gear and the car pulled away from the curb.

'She seems nice,' said Elizabeth, taking her eyes away from the road for a second to cast a flawless smile back at Morris.

'Yeah,' agreed Sandra Coughlin from the passenger seat, her voice muffled by a mouthful of corned beef. 'This is great!'

'Jewish mother,' grinned Morris. 'It doesn't surprise me that you blue-blooded, Mount Holyoake WASPs have never tasted good deli food.'

'Who are you calling a WASP, Amherst boy?' replied Sandra in mock indignation. 'I'm one hundred per cent Boston bog Irish.'

'Southie, eh?' joked Morris.

'You'd better believe it,' grinned Sandra.

'Okay, okay,' interjected Elizabeth. 'Instead of refighting the wars of religion, why don't you do something useful and tell me the shortest route to the New England Thruway?'

'Take the second left,' Morris instructed.

The trio allowed three days to travel the thirteen hundred miles from Boston to Selma. But with a driver pool of three, the journey was manageable. They stayed overnight at motels in Hagerstown, Maryland, and Knoxville, Tennessee, pulling into Selma at around five in the afternoon of day three—6 March 1965.

Asking directions from a passing African American woman, they found their way to the Brown African Methodist Episcopal Church on Sylvan Street.

Elizabeth giggled as the trio made its way towards the front door of the church. 'Don't worry, they aren't going to burn you at the stake as a heretic.'

Morris laughed in embarrassment. 'Is it that obvious?'

Sandy laughed. 'You look as out of place as a rabbi at a best bacon contest.'

'Cut me some slack. It's the first time I've ever been in a church.' And this one looked imposing, with its towers, arches and white stone trim.

A dozen or so people were in the midst of a discussion. A silver-haired, African American matron who appeared to be in her sixties hustled towards them. 'Halloo thar,' she said, smiling broadly. 'I'm Rosa-May Johnson. Welcome to Brown AME, or African Methodist Episcopal if you want to be proper.'

'Hi,' replied Elizabeth. I'm Elizabeth Willoughby, and this is Sandra Coughlin and Morris Glazen. We're here for the march.'

'And where're you from?' asked Rosa-May.

'Boston,' replied Sandra.

'My, my, you've come all the way from Boston,' Rosa-May echoed. 'You must be tired and hungry.'

'We could eat,' grinned Elizabeth.

Rosa-May turned towards the table where discussions were ongoing. 'John, come over here and meet these fine people who have come all the way from Boston to march with us.'

A young, dark-skinned man rose from the table and approached.

'Hello,' he said in a deep voice that resonated with a Southern drawl. 'Ah'm John Lewis of the Student Non-Violent Coordinating Committee. Ah'm pleased to make your acquaintance.'

'It's an honour,' replied Morris, grasping the hand Lewis extended in greeting.

Lewis turned to Rosa-May. 'These good folk have come a long way to help out. I think it's only fair that we offer them a li'l Southern hospitality for the night, don't you think?'

'No, really,' said Morris, his hands raised, palms outward. 'We don't want to impose. We'll find a couple of motels ...'

'Are you tryin' to insult me, young man?' Rosa-May challenged with a frown.

'N ... no, ma'am.'

'Then it's settled,' said Rosa-May with a decisive nod.

'I have other matters to attend to,' said Lewis, 'so I'll leave our guests in your capable hands, Rosa-May. I hope to see you all tomorrow.'

Lewis walked back to his place at the table as Rosa-May turned towards the trio.

'There are showers and a bathroom in the back of the church. So y'all freshen up and then we'll go over to my house for dinner. I have a spare room for the young ladies and you ... Mr Glazen, was it?'

Morris nodded.

'Mr Glazen can sleep on the couch.'

'Thank you, Mrs Johnson,' said Elizabeth with a sweet smile.

'That's all right, darlin',' replied Rosa-May, giving Elizabeth a pat on the hand. 'Y'all run along now and clean yourselves up.'

Morris allowed the girls to shower first, passing the time until they emerged slogging through a dog-eared copy of Camus's *La Peste* in its original French.

When Morris emerged from the shower, Rosa-May Johnson led the trio around the corner to a modest, weatherboard home with a small, yet immaculate, front garden.

'I love your roses,' said Sandra, as they walked up the path to Rosa-May's front verandah.

Rosa-May beamed. 'Thank you, darlin'. They're my pride and joy. Sit yourselves down in the livin' room,' she said, once they'd entered.

Morris took a seat on a frayed couch while Elizabeth and Sandra insisted on helping with dinner.

He was another twenty-five pages through *La Peste* when Rosa-May came through from the kitchen.

'The girls tell me you don't eat pork,' she said.

Morris shrugged. 'I'll be fine with whatever.'

'Well, just to be on the safe side, I'm cooking up some fried chicken and collard greens. To give you a taste of Alabama.'

And what a taste it was. The meal was nothing like the Eastern European fare of his childhood. Morris ate his fill, and then ate some more, much to the delight of Rosa-May and the amused approval of Elizabeth and Sandra.

The soundest of sleeps followed.

The next day—7 March—began back at Brown AME, with a non-denominational prayer for the soul of Jimmie Lee Jackson. Jackson, a black civil rights activist, had been shot to death a month before in nearby Marion, Alabama, by a state trooper.

Morris snapped a few shots of the people at prayer and left the church, wanting to be well positioned to get photos of the crowd as it assembled for the march.

He was well into his second roll of film by the time the march kicked off. Locating Elizabeth and Sandra several rows behind the front rank of protesters, Morris made his way through the crowd to join them.

'How many people?' Morris asked Elizabeth.

'I dunno,' she replied with a shrug. 'Five hundred, maybe? Sandra?'

'I'd say six,' Sandra replied.

They were now proceeding away from the church.

'Where's Martin Luther King?' asked Elizabeth.

Morris shrugged. 'I thought he was going to be here too.'

'He's in Atlanta,' volunteered a tall black man in his thirties who was walking beside them. 'The Reverend Hosea Williams from the Southern Christian Leadership Conference and John Lewis from the SNCC are leading us today.'

'Thanks,' smiled Sandra and the man nodded.

The marchers made their way down Selma Avenue and turned left into Broad Street. Morris could see the curved iron trusses of a bridge in the distance.

'What's that?' Morris asked his black neighbour, pointing to the bridge.

'I'm Matthew Williams, pastor at Dexter Avenue Baptist in Montgomery,' he said, extending his hand.

Morris flushed. 'Oh, sorry. I'm Morris Glazen from Amherst College.'

'That's in Massachusetts, I believe.'

Morris nodded.

'Welcome to the struggle.'

'Thank you, Reverend,' replied Elizabeth.

'And the bridge?' Morris gestured towards the span that was now only a couple of hundred yards away.

'That, my friends, is Edmund Pettus Bridge across the Alabama River, named after a former colonel in the Confederate Army, a United States senator and Grand Dragon of the Ku Klux Klan.'

'Naming a public bridge after such a man is disgusting,' said Sandra with a frown.

'You haven't spent much time in Alabama, my dear,' replied Williams with a cynical smile.

Morris inspected the iron truss lattice work that supported the bridge as they marched beneath it.

But then, suddenly, the column of demonstrators came to a halt.

'What's going on?' asked Elizabeth.

Another smile from Williams. 'I think you're about to be introduced to another part of Alabama reality.'

He pointed ahead towards where a phalanx of white-helmeted and gas-masked Alabama state troopers was advancing in step, their billy clubs slapping their hands in rhythm with every stride.

The order to halt was sounded and the troopers halted about fifty yards short of the demonstrators' front row. Arrayed behind the state troopers were other law enforcement officers, some of them mounted. Then, behind the local sheriff's deputies, a crowd of segregationists waved Confederate battle flags.

The metallic tones of an Alabama drawl amplified by a battery-powered loudspeaker cut through the air.

'This is Major John Cloud of the Alabama State Police. By the authority vested in him as governor of Alabama, Governor George Wallace has declared this to be an illegal assembly. Y'all have two minutes to disperse before we will be forced to take action.'

Peering over the heads and shoulders of those in front of him, Morris could see the figure of John Lewis standing still in the front row of marchers.

'Major Cloud, can we have a word?' said a man next to John Lewis, who Morris later learned was Reverend Hosea Williams.

'No, you have two minutes to disperse,' replied Major Cloud in a tone of clear contempt.

'Can I have a word?' pleaded Williams.

Cloud shook his head. 'There will be no word. Disperse or face the consequences.'

Morris cast a nervous glance at his watch, but midway

through the wait the troopers suddenly charged into the ranks of marchers.

Chaos ensued as demonstrators rushed backwards to escape the swinging clubs and the tear-gas canisters being thrown by police. Mounted troopers charged into the crowd, trampling people underfoot.

The press of fleeing marchers knocked Elizabeth down. Morris kneeled to help her, but was struck on the back of the head and collapsed on top of her.

By the time he regained consciousness, the tumult of violence and pain had flowed past them. Helping Elizabeth to her feet, he looked on in horror as the ranks of state troopers and police pummelled the demonstrators into the streets of Selma. 'Where's Sandra?' Elizabeth said.

'Come on,' Morris said, taking Elizabeth by the hand. 'We need to take cover. We'll look for her later.' The two of them hurried to the southern end of the bridge where they sought shelter amongst a thick stand of trees and shrubs.

'Morris, you've been hurt,' said Elizabeth in a shocked voice. 'The whole back of your head is covered in blood!'

'I'm fine,' Morris said, although his head ached horribly. 'Scalps bleed a lot, or so I've been told.'

'Fine, my ass,' she barked. 'You're going to let me have a look at it. Now sit still.'

Morris did his best to comply as he felt her fingers probing the back of his head, although he did hiss and flinch once or twice.

He suddenly remembered the camera hanging around his neck. 'Shit,' he said after a cursory examination. 'The lens is broken.'

'I'm more concerned about where you're broken,' she announced.

'I think you're going to need stitches.' She flashed him a smile. 'I haven't thanked you.'

'For what?' asked Morris, his mind still fuzzy.

'For saving me back there, silly. You were very brave.'

Then Elizabeth Willoughby did something that Morris had often dreamed about, but never expected. She leaned over and kissed him. Not a chaste peck on the cheek, but a real kiss.

'Wow,' was all Morris could say when they drew apart.

Elizabeth grinned. 'I thought an English major might be a bit more eloquent.'

'How's this for eloquence?' Morris asked as he placed his hand behind her head and kissed her again.

Suddenly, they were in no hurry to pass over the bridge to the Selma side of the river. But after a while, Elizabeth stood up and began buttoning her blouse.

'We'd better get back,' she said. 'I'm worried about Sandra, and she'll be worried about us.'

'You're right,' said Morris. 'I ... I forgot about her, I'm ashamed to say.'

Hand in hand, they made their way back across the Edmund Pettus Bridge, lowering their eyes before the belligerent glares of state troopers and white civilians waving Confederate flags.

Arriving at Rosa-May's house, they knocked on the door, but there was no answer.

They made their way around the corner to Brown AME where Sandra fell upon them with a shriek of relief.

'I was so worried, you guys!' she said. Her hand then shot to her mouth as she noticed the matted blood on Morris's head and neck.

'Rosa-May! Morris has been hurt!'

Rosa-May Johnson rushed over and took Morris by the hand. 'Are you all right?'

'I'm fine, thank you,' Morris replied. 'But Elizabeth thinks I might need stiches.'

'You come with me. Dr Casey is over there treating some of the people who were hurt.'

'Hmm,' murmured Dr Casey as he examined Morris's head. 'I think four stiches will do the trick. But I'm going to have to shave part of your head.'

Morris grinned in response. 'It'll make me look like one of those friars. Perhaps next time they won't knock me out if they think I'm a priest.'

'Don't bank on it,' said the doctor grimly.

Forty minutes later, Morris was ready to go, stitches and shaved head included. The three college students then walked back with Rosa-May to her house where they collected their belongings and Elizabeth phoned her parents, asking them to call Morris and Sandra's family as well. Morris insisted on paying for the call.

'I'm sorry we have to leave so soon,' Elizabeth apologised, 'but our parents will be worried. I'm sure they've seen the news on TV, and with fifty-eight people hurt, they'll want to see for themselves that we're all right.'

'I understand,' replied Rosa-May with a wistful smile. 'But they also have a lot to be proud of. You three give me hope that America can be a better place one day.'

Rosa-May Johnson escorted her guests out to Elizabeth's Mustang and within a couple of minutes they were ready to go. She kissed each of the three on the cheek and Elizabeth waved and drove away.

The two girls didn't allow Morris to drive, so when Sandra was at the wheel Elizabeth joined him in the back, where they cuddled.

'You're a couple of thoughtless bastards,' Sarah announced with a smile that defused the insult. 'There I was, terrified that you were both dead. Now I understand that you guys were in no hurry to get back at all.'

The only response Elizabeth could make was the upraised middle finger she flashed at her friend. Her mouth was otherwise engaged.

END NOTE

In the annals of the American civil rights movement, 7 March 1965 became known as 'Bloody Sunday'. For the first time, the sheer brutality of the segregationist South's enforcement of Jim Crow was brought into living rooms throughout America via the family television set.

Things moved swiftly after Bloody Sunday. Martin Luther King hastened to Selma from Atlanta. With his trademark cadences, he called on 'religious leaders from all over the nation to join us on Tuesday in our peaceful, nonviolent march for freedom.'

Rabbis, priests, pastors and ministers from across the nation answered the call. King and other civil rights leaders announced plans to stage a second Selma to Montgomery procession on 9 March. But Federal District Court Judge Frank M Johnson gave notice that he intended to issue a restraining order prohibiting the march until at least 11 March. Martin Luther King received a call from the White House in which President Johnson urged that the march should be postponed until a federal court order could provide protection for the protesters.

Pending this court order, King consulted with John Doar,

the Deputy Assistant Attorney-General for Civil Rights. The consensus view among the civil rights leaders in Selma was to decline the president's request for a delay and proceed with the planned protest on the afternoon of 9 March.

That day, King led more than two thousand people, including hundreds of ministers, priests, rabbis and social activists, along the same route taken by the Bloody Sunday marchers two days earlier.

Upon reaching the site of Sunday's attack, King stopped and asked his fellow protesters to kneel and pray. King believed that the Alabama state troopers arrayed at the scene were eager for another confrontation that would increase the likelihood of a federal injunction prohibiting the march. He wasn't inclined to play the segregationists' game.

After prayers, the marchers rose, and Martin Luther King led them back into Selma, avoiding another eruption of police violence and skirting the issue of whether to obey Judge Johnson's court order.

Unaware of Martin Luther King's legal–political stratagem, some of the younger demonstrators were critical of the decision not to push on to Montgomery, but the plan worked.

This exhibition of restraint in the face of violence induced President Johnson to issue a public statement of support in which he declared, 'Americans everywhere join in deploring the brutality with which a number of negro citizens of Alabama were treated when they sought to dramatise their deep and sincere interest in attaining the precious right to vote.' Johnson went on to promise the introduction of a voting rights bill to Congress within a few days.

That same evening, several local whites in Selma attacked James Reeb, a white Unitarian minister from Massachusetts who had come to participate in the protest. His death two days later generated rising national concern over the situation in Alabama. President Johnson personally telephoned his condolences to Reeb's widow and pressured Alabama Governor George Wallace to protect demonstrators and support universal suffrage.

By complete coincidence, the American ABC network premiered the film *Judgement at Nuremberg* on the evening of that same Sunday 7 March. An estimated 48 million people tuned in to watch the film, which dealt with the moral and legal culpability of those who had perpetrated Nazi war crimes. Shortly after the movie started, ABC management decided to interrupt the film with a special report from Selma.

Viewers who may have been superficially aware of the demonstrations were now confronted with visual evidence of the brutality and violence of the police at Selma. The media had been regularly reporting since January on standoffs between blacks who wanted to register to vote and Selma's racist sheriff, Jim Clark, but now television coverage triggered national outrage.

Two years earlier, the nation had been scandalised by the sight of Birmingham Commissioner of Public Safety, 'Bull' Connor, deploying police dogs and high-powered fire hoses against nonviolent civil rights protesters. In response, President Kennedy promoted the famous *Civil Rights Act of 1964* that outlawed Jim Crow segregation by race.

But even the Bull Connor firehose footage didn't shake the American national psyche the way images from Bloody Sunday in Selma did.

In large, part of this was sheer happenstance. The special ABC Selma report interrupted a primetime broadcast and the footage from Selma thematically complemented the showing of *Judgment at Nuremberg*.

In the days following the broadcast, several members of Congress took to the floor of the House of Representatives to liken Alabama Governor George Wallace to Hitler and his state police to Nazi storm troopers.

'I just witnessed on television the new sequel to Adolf Hitler's brown shirts,' one person wrote to *The Birmingham News*. Another person wrote, 'The scene in Alabama looked like scenes on an old newsreel of Germany in the 1930s.'

One Selma shopkeeper allowed himself to be quoted anonymously about the institutional racism of Jim Crow. 'Everybody knows it's going on, but they try to pretend they don't see it. I saw *Judgement at Nuremberg* last night and I thought it fits right in; it's just like Selma.'

John Lewis, now recovered from the beating he suffered at the hands of Alabama state troopers, said, 'I don't see how President Johnson can send troops to Vietnam, I don't see how he can send troops to the Congo, I don't see how he can send troops to Africa and can't send troops to Selma.'

On 15 March, President Johnson delivered a special message to Congress in which he declared, 'There is no negro problem. There is no Southern problem. There is no Northern problem. There is only an American problem. Their cause must be our cause too. Because it is not just negroes, but really it is all of us who must overcome the crippling legacy of bigotry and injustice. And we shall overcome.'

The following day, Selma demonstrators submitted a proposal to Judge Johnson, who approved the march and enjoined Governor Wallace and local law enforcement officers to refrain from harassing or threatening demonstrators.

After five days and fifty miles, Martin Luther King and his

followers arrived at the steps of the Alabama State Capitol in Montgomery on 25 March 1965. By this point, the number of marchers had swelled to 25,000. Included in the crowd were Assistant Attorneys General John Doar and Ramsey Clark, and former Assistant Attorney-General Burke Marshall. They were met in Montgomery by 50,000 additional people of all races and creeds.

'There never was a moment in American history more honourable and more inspiring than the pilgrimage of clergymen and laymen of every race and faith pouring into Selma to face danger at the side of its embattled negroes,' declared King. He went on to proclaim that, 'the end we seek is a society at peace with itself, a society that can live with its conscience. And that will be a day not of the white man, not of the black man. That will be the day of man as man.'

But such a day was yet to come. That same night, a housewife from Michigan named Viola Liuzzo, who had come to Alabama as a volunteer, was shot and killed by four members of the Ku Klux Klan, one of whom was an undercover agent for the FBI. Deputy Attorney-General Doar prosecuted three Klansmen for conspiring to violate her civil rights.

Soon after the completion of the march, a delegation of leaders was rebuffed by Governor Wallace when they attempted to deliver a petition to the Alabama governor's mansion.

But progress went on nonetheless. On 6 August, six months after Bloody Sunday, President Johnson signed into law the *Voting Rights Act of 1965*, with Martin Luther King, Jr, and other civil rights leaders standing behind him.

This legislation banned literacy tests as a requirement for voting and mandated federal oversight of voter registration in areas where such tests had been abused to deny African Americans the vote. It also charged the US attorney-general with the duty to challenge the use of poll taxes for state and local elections.

Along with the *Civil Rights Act of 1964*, the *Voting Rights Act of 1965* was one of the most expansive pieces of civil rights legislation in American history. It greatly reduced the disparity between black and white voters in the US and allowed greater numbers of African Americans to participate in politics and government at the local, state and national levels.

In his annual address to the Southern Christian Leadership Conference a few days later, King noted, 'Montgomery led to the *Civil Rights Act of 1957* and 1960; Birmingham inspired the *Civil Rights Act of 1964*; and Selma produced the Voting Rights legislation of 1965.'

In retrospect, it is quite clear that Bloody Sunday in Selma was a tipping point in America's civil rights struggle.

Top left: Alabama police attack Selma to Montgomery marchers, known as 'Bloody Sunday,' in 1965

Top right: Marchers on street in Harlem, New York City, in 1965

Bottom left: Participants in the Selma to Montgomery march in Alabama in 1965

Bottom right: Dr Martin Luther King, Dr Ralph David Abernathy, their families and others leading the Selma to Montgomery march in 1965

7. THE ASSASSINATION OF MARTIN LUTHER KING, JR

4 April 1968

James Doherty III was presiding over his family's customary evening meal when the phone rang.

'I'll get it!' Meade, his fourteen-year-old daughter, assumed all phone calls were for her.

'It's for you, Dad,' she yelled a few moments later.

Doherty followed his daughter into the kitchen and took the receiver.

'This is Doherty.'

'Jim, it's Simon.' Special Agent Simon Quinn, a colleague at the Criminal Intelligence Division of FBI Headquarters, needed no further introduction. 'You know that Martin Luther King, Jr, was assassinated earlier this evening?'

'What?' Doherty exclaimed.

'Yeah, you heard me.' The voice was grave. 'Where have you been for the past three hours?'

'Playing Monopoly with Arlene and the girls.'

'Right. Well, King was shot with a long gun at his motel in Memphis.'

'Shit!' cursed Doherty. 'Just like Kennedy.'

'Yep, just like Kennedy,' Simon echoed.

Doherty felt a presence behind him and turned to see his wife, Arlene, and his twin daughters eavesdropping, their expressions concerned.

'So, what's our next move?' asked Doherty.

'Hoover has put together a special taskforce and he asked for you by name. So, pack a bag and get yourself to Andrews by 6 am tomorrow. The air force has laid on a C-141 for a direct flight to Memphis. There'll be twenty-five of us and a forensics team with their equipment.'

'Right. See you there.'

Doherty hung up the phone and turned to face his wife and daughters, his expression grim. 'Martin Luther King, Jr, was assassinated earlier this evening.'

'Oh!' The cry of dismay came from three mouths in unison. The two girls, Meade and Debra, began to sob as Arlene moved to comfort them.

'I'm going in to switch on the news,' said Doherty. 'We should all go in to watch.'

'Don't you think the girls are upset enough?' challenged Arlene.

Doherty cast a sombre look at wife. 'They need to see this, honey. This is one of those terrible moments in history that they'll remember all their lives.'

Arlene nodded and the family went into the living room where they watched a special report by Walter Cronkite of CBS. Both his wife and daughters were weeping and Doherty made discreet attempts to wipe his own moist eyes.

An hour later, after the TV was shut off, he informed Arlene and the girls of his summons to service.

'I hope you're the one to catch the bastard who did this,' growled Debra.

'Language!' chided Arlene.

'We'll let the foul mouth slide, just this once,' said Doherty in a tone of mild reproof. 'But I'll do my best. Come and give me a kiss before you go off to bed.'

Meade and Debra dutifully hugged their father, and received kisses on the head in return before trailing off to their bedrooms.

He cast a questioning glance at his wife as she got up to leave the living room.

'Where are you going, honey?'

She turned and he saw the sad smile on her face. 'If you have to be at Andrews by zero six, I'd better pack your things.'

He followed his wife into the bedroom where they filled a battered, leather suitcase with a week's worth of clothing and other personal items.

Arising at 4 am he traversed the thirty miles separating his home in Falls Church, Virginia, and Andrews Air Force Base, Maryland, in little more than half an hour. Flashing his FBI credentials to the guards at the gate, he was directed to a hangar at the north-east corner of the facility.

Doherty parked his car and showed his credentials to another air force security policeman posted at the hangar entrance. Stepping though the door, he nodded to colleagues who were chatting in small groups over cups of coffee as another group of men were arranging an easel in front of several rows of benches.

Gravitating to a table with a coffee urn, Doherty poured himself a cup. He was just beginning to feel invigorated by the caffeine coursing through his system when a man he recognised as Associate Deputy Director Simpson called the group to order.

'All right, let's everybody sit down and I'll bring you up to speed,' Simpson announced in a loud voice.

Doherty saw Simon Quinn waving from the second-row bench and walked over to join him. 'Quite the party,' he whispered as the benches around them quickly filled. The chatter faded and Doherty noted the looks of anticipation on the faces of his colleagues.

Simpson waited until complete silence settled across the hangar and then nodded.

'Most of you know me, but for those who don't, my name is Arthur Simpson and I am Associate Deputy FBI Director in the Office of Director Hoover. Now, unless you've been living in a cave, you're all aware of what happened in Memphis yesterday. I've been instructed by the director to assemble a team that will augment the resources of the Memphis field office. You constitute that team and I will be in overall command. All contact with Washington will go through me and me alone. Any questions so far?'

Simpson paused, but his audience remained silent.

'So, here's what we know. The Reverend Martin Luther King, Jr, was killed by a single round fired from a rifle at a range of less than a hundred yards. The presumed murder weapon—a scoped Remington 760 pump action—was found shortly afterwards together with a pair of binoculars and fifty rounds of .30-06 ammunition. Those items are now in the Memphis PD lab, and Dr Feldman and his team will assume responsibility for all forensic analysis.'

'And what will the locals say about that?' asked Feldman, a scholarly, bespectacled man in his fifties.

'They'll say "Yes, Sir" to a direct request from the White House,' grinned Simpson as a gust of laughter swept through the room.

'Now settle down, people,' chided Simpson. 'This is a very serious business. Rioting has broken out in cities throughout the country. We need to solve this crime and soon. The eyes of all Americans will be focused on us. Now we'll be boarding the C-141 outside, which the air force has been kind enough to put at our disposal. Any questions?'

Nobody spoke and the FBI personnel left the hangar and walked to the open rear ramp of the C-141. Selecting a vacant spot on thick, red, webbing benches that ran the length of the cargo compartment on either side, Doherty drew on a skill he'd developed years earlier as a marine—the ability to sleep anywhere.

He was awakened by the popping of his ears as the plane began its descent into Memphis. Doherty glanced at his watch. Two hours and eleven minutes since take-off. There was a sudden rumble as the landing gear descended. Within a few minutes, the transport plane touched down and taxied to a secluded corner of the airport. The FBI team quickly loaded their equipment onto a waiting bus that drove to a large five-storey, greystone building with the words 'Memphis Police Station' etched above four Ionic stone columns flanking its entrance.

'Follow me,' Simpson said as he disembarked. 'We've been allocated the entire north wing of the first floor. That's where the forensic lab is located; so, Dr Feldman, that'll be your stamping ground.'

The scientist nodded and Simpson led the way through the building to a large office with desks and noticeboards fixed to the walls. A big blackboard with a large-scale map of Memphis was positioned at the front of the room.

Some of the desks were occupied by men in button-down white shirts and ties who were talking on the telephone. Another white-shirted trio was posting photographs, schematics and other documents on one of the boards.

'Hi, Greg,' Simpson called in a familiar tone as one of the noticeboard posters approached the group.

The two shook hands and then Simpson turned to his Washington counterpart. 'Gents, this is Greg Hanson, the SAC of the Memphis office. He'll bring us up to speed on the latest.'

'Okay, everyone, take a seat and listen up,' announced Hanson in a nasal voice that seemed incongruous in view of his six-foot-six-inch height and NFL line-backer build. 'I'd like to introduce Deputy Chief for Investigations, Walter Bayley, of the Memphis Police.'

An overweight man who appeared to be in his fifties stepped forward from the blackboard to stand beside Hanson.

'Chief Bayley, why don't you fill our Washington DC contingent in on where we are at present?'

Bayley nodded. 'Thank you, Special-Agent-in-Charge Hanson,' he said in a deep, Southern drawl. 'So, here's what we know. Dr King arrived yesterday afternoon and checked into the Lorraine Motel, the place he'd always stay when in town. The media was all over his visit like ticks on a hound. His location was the worst kept secret in Memphis.'

'And this visit had to do with the Sanitation Workers Strike?' asked Doherty.

'And you are?'

'Sorry, James Doherty, Supervisory Special Agent, FBI Criminal Intelligence Division.'

'Chief Bayley is well acquainted with my team from the Memphis office,' interjected Hanson, 'but from now on it would be a good idea if everyone asking a question identifies himself.'

Bayley nodded his agreement. 'The answer to Mr Doherty's question is, yes. Are you out-of-towners familiar with the strike?'

A flurry of heads shook.

'In February this year, two Memphis garbage collectors were crushed to death in a work accident. There's been simmering resentment among the garbage workers about their pay and working conditions for a while now.'

'Special Agent Barns, Washington Field Office,' interjected a fresh-faced young man who looked to be barely out of high school. 'And I assume the majority of sanitation workers are negro?'

Bayley's face flushed. 'They're all coloured folk.'

'But back to the history,' interjected Hanson, to deflect any further embarrassment. 'Two years ago, Memphis sanitation workers went on strike, but it petered out after a few weeks. This time, those two deaths attracted much broader public support. When more than 1,300 Memphis city sanitation workers walked off the job last February, they were joined by a coalition of 150 local clergy.'

Doherty raised his hand and received a nod of acknowledgement from Hanson.

'Martin Luther King, Jr, is … was based in Atlanta? How did he play into this?'

'We were just coming to that,' said Hanson, with just a hint of annoyance. 'Chief Bayley, do you want to answer?'

Bayley cleared his throat. 'The leader of that local clergy group here in Memphis is Reverend James Lawson. He sent word to his friend, Dr Martin Luther King, Jr, with a request for assistance. Dr King answered the call and a couple of weeks ago he spoke to a crowd of between fifteen and twenty thousand at one of the big negro churches here in town—Mason Temple. He made a second trip to Memphis ten days later to join Lawson in a march on behalf of the striking sanitation workers, but this time a group of protesters broke off from the main body and began to loot nearby businesses. Police responded with tear gas and baton charges. In the melee that followed, a sixteen-year-old boy was shot and killed by a Memphis police officer.'

'What date was that, sir?' asked Barns, a pen poised over an open notebook on his lap.

'It was the 28th of March,' Hanson replied. 'Some witnesses said the looters were affiliated with the local Black Panther Party, but the Panthers denied it; so I'm sure they're completely innocent.'

Hanson's cynical grin triggered a spate of guffaws from the mixed group of FBI agents and Memphis cops.

'In any event,' Hanson continued, 'Dr King returned to Atlanta. We've been told by his colleagues at the Southern Christian Leadership Conference that he felt embarrassed by the violence on the 28th. He considered not returning to Memphis, but then he came to the conclusion that the Sanitation Workers Strike aligned perfectly with his latest advocacy initiative. Something he called the Poor People's Campaign. So, on the afternoon of 3 April, Dr King and his entourage checked into the Lorraine Motel. Questions so far?'

Hanson paused for a few moments, and seeing no raised hands nodded to Deputy Chief Bayley.

'We've been told that Dr King was not feeling well,' Bayley continued, 'but he still delivered a speech at the Mason Temple to an audience of two thousand people, and by all accounts it was a stem-winder.'

'If I may, Chief Bayley,' interposed Hanson, 'I'd like to read from a newspaper article about the speech, in which King said, "I've been to the mountaintop and seen the Promised Land". For reasons that will be pretty obvious, I think that name is going to stick.'

Dr King spoke for forty minutes in a wide-ranging speech that described the Memphis sanitation strike as yet another chapter in a long struggle for economic justice. He invoked the New Testament parable of the Good Samaritan to urge civic involvement and told the story of the 1958 attempt on his life when a deranged woman stabbed him with a letter opener. But it was the closing segment that caused Dr King's speech to go down in history as one of his greatest:

> I have seen the Promised Land. I may not get there with you. But I want you to know tonight, that we, as a people, will get to the Promised Land. And I'm happy tonight. I'm not worried about anything. I'm not fearing any man. Mine eyes have seen the glory of the coming of the Lord.

Hanson looked up in silence from the newspaper, his eyes glistening with tears. Doherty glanced around and was surprised to see many of his most hard-bitten FBI colleagues were wiping their eyes as well.

Arthur Simpson stepped forward. 'Thank you, Greg. I don't have to explain the raw combustible power of those words when combined with this terrible event. As we speak, rioting has broken out across the country. And it doesn't help that Mrs King is saying her husband was warned that a price had been placed on his head.'

'Did that warning come from us?' asked Doherty.

Simpson nodded. 'Yes. The Atlanta SAC contacted him personally about ten days ago, but our intelligence was based on background chatter and we had no specifics.'

'That won't be worth a tinker's damn to the black community,' observed Doherty.

Simpson nodded. 'Absolutely right. It won't. Which is why we have to solve this case ASAP. Gentleman, I want you to pull out all the stops. You'll be operating in teams of two, one FBI agent matched with a detective from the MPD Homicide Unit. Let me be absolutely clear. I expect seamless cooperation between our agencies. That means no foolish competitions about seniority or authority. This investigation is too important and Chief Bayley and I will have zero tolerance for distractions of any kind. Are we clear?'

There was a general murmur of assent.

'Right, then. Senior Special Agent Watson will roster you into teams.'

A youngish man standing behind Hanson waved his clipboard.

'Let's get to it,' ordered Simpson. 'Doherty, to me.'

Doherty approached his superior. 'Yes, sir.'

'Jim, you'll be posted here at MPD. I may have to fly back to DC to brief Director Hoover and the White House. So, I want you working directly with me and the chief, here. You'll be the FBI's point man if I have to leave.'

'Yes, sir,' replied Doherty as he extended a hand to Bayley. 'Pleased to meet you, sir.'

'Likewise,' replied Bayley as he accepted the offered hand. 'Associate Deputy Director Simpson has told me good things about you.'

'What's the lab telling us, sir?' asked Doherty.

Bayley grimaced. 'The .03-06 round taken from the body has been matched to the Remington found near the scene. Documents in the bundle containing the rifle implicated three men—Eric Starvo Galt, Harvey Lowmeyer and John Willard, but only one set of prints have been found, so we think that might be deliberate misinformation.'

'And the prints are being run now?'

'Yes, they've been sent to the FBI and state police throughout the country. We're hoping for a match soon.'

'What about eyewitnesses?'

'There are multiple accounts that describe a single white man hurrying away from a rooming house directly across the street from the Lorraine Motel to a white Ford Mustang parked nearby. We have an APB out for the Mustang.'

'That's good,' said Doherty. 'Can't be too many of those around Memphis. And the rooming house is where the shot was fired from?'

'Yeah,' replied Bayley. 'It's called Bessie Brewer's. Some of Dr King's associates were able to identify the direction of the shot and we found a single shell casing near a bathroom window with a clear line of sight to the balcony of the Lorraine. Residents of the rooming house also report hearing footsteps in the bathroom just before the shot was fired.'

'Is there an autopsy report?'

'Provisional,' replied Simpson as he picked up a manila folder on a desk to his right and began to read:

> A single .30-06 calibre bullet struck the right side of Dr King's face, cracking his jawbone. It exited his lower face and re-entered his body through the neck area, severing several arteries and shattering his spine. Dr King's associates and one of Chief Bayley's undercover officers tried to stem the bleeding with a towel until an ambulance arrived. He was taken to St Joseph's Hospital where doctors performed emergency surgery. Dr King was pronounced dead at 7.05 pm.

Simpson closed the folder and looked up with a sombre frown.

*

James Doherty spent the next two days coordinating the collection of witness statements and forensic evidence. After a telephone consultation with Arthur Simpson, the Washington DC team and all the forensic analysts boarded another air force transport plane for the trip back to Andrews Air Force Base.

A special section of FBI Headquarters in the Department of Justice Building was set aside to accommodate the ad hoc King assassination task force. James Doherty was appointed Arthur Simpson's second-in-command. It was there he received word that a white Ford Mustang had been discovered by police in Atlanta. Fingerprint analysis quickly revealed that the car's driver and the Memphis shooter were one and the same person.

Meanwhile, it seemed as though the entire United States had ground to a halt. Democrats and Republicans alike suspended their campaigns during that presidential election year. The Academy Awards ceremony was postponed. Businesses, schools and other public buildings were closed. The day Doherty returned to Washington—7 April—was declared a national day of mourning by President Lyndon Johnson.

Meanwhile, predominantly black, inner-city neighbourhoods across the United States exploded in a paroxysm of violence. More than one hundred American cities saw major outbreaks of rioting, arson, looting and violence. In all, 27,000 people were arrested, about 3,500 were injured and more than forty were killed. In Washington DC alone, 6,100 people were arrested and more than a thousand were injured, while in Chicago there were 125 fires and eleven deaths.

Indianapolis was one of the few major American metropolitan areas where a major outbreak of violence did not occur. Some attribute this forbearance to Democratic presidential candidate Robert Kennedy, who was on a campaign stop in the city when news of Dr King's death became known. That same night,

4 April, Kennedy spoke to a mostly black audience at an inner-city rally:

> For those of you who are black and are tempted to be filled with hatred and distrust at the injustice of such an act, against all white people, I can only say that I feel in my own heart the same kind of feeling. I had a member of my family killed, but he was killed by a white man. But we have to make an effort in the United States, we have to make an effort to understand, to go beyond these rather difficult times.

Robert Kennedy's Indianapolis speech was the first time since November 1963 he had spoken publicly about the assassination of his brother, President John F Kennedy. Like Indianapolis, Atlanta also remained mostly peaceful, in large part due to the efforts of students and faculty at historically black Atlanta University Consortium who acted as peacekeeping marshals in honour of Dr King's doctrine of nonviolence.

On 9 April 1968, Doherty and his team watched from the special taskforce office at FBI headquarters as all three television networks cancelled their normal schedules to broadcast the Martin Luther King, Jr, funeral in Atlanta.

Standing outside Dr King's Ebenezer Baptist Church, CBS correspondent Morley Safer read from his notes to describe the private funeral service held within:

> Dr King's friend and colleague, Reverend Ralph Abernathy, commenced proceedings by declaring it to be 'one of the darkest

hours of mankind', intoned Safer. A tape recording was then played of a speech that King delivered two months earlier describing the manner in which he'd hoped to be remembered: 'I'd like somebody to mention that day, that Martin Luther King, Jr, tried to give his life serving others. I'd like for somebody to say that day, that Martin Luther King, Jr, tried to love somebody. Yes, if you want to say that I was a drum major, say that I was a drum major for justice. Say that I was a drum major for peace. I was a drum major for righteousness. And all the other shallow things will not matter.'

Doherty once again felt tears welling up in his eyes as he watched the King family, friends and dignitaries leave the church for the funeral procession. He noted the presence of all four leading presidential candidates—Democrats Robert Kennedy, Eugene McCarthy and Vice President Hubert Humphrey, and Republican Richard Nixon.

'I wouldn't want to be the Secret Service agent in charge of that protection detail,' said Simon Quinn, shaking his head.

Doherty grimaced. 'Don't even think it, Simon. Don't even think it.'

The FBI agents watched as the television cameras followed the funeral cortege through streets lined with thousands of silent mourners. More cameras had been set up on the grounds of Dr King's alma mater, Morehouse College, where an outdoor public service was to be held.

Morehouse President Emeritus Benjamin May spoke, and blues singer Mahalia Jackson moved onlookers and millions of others in the television audience to tears with her rendition of the gospel classic, 'Precious Lord'.

The following week passed in a blur for James Doherty as he

worked eighteen-hour days and slept on an army cot in his office at FBI headquarters. The closest he came to seeing his family was every evening when Arlene and the twins would visit the Department of Justice Building with a fresh change of clothing.

A big break in the case came on 19 April, when the FBI crime lab identified the common fingerprints on the Remington rifle, binoculars, rounds of .30-06 ammunition and the Ford Mustang. The presumed assassin was a forty-year-old prison escapee named James Earl Ray.

Doherty snapped up the file on Ray and began to read:

> Burglary, armed robbery and mail fraud. Escaped from the Missouri State Penitentiary in the back of a bread van. Interviews with former cellmates revealed that Ray was a rabid white supremacist who despised Martin Luther King. The sight of Dr King on television, reported one fellow inmate, was enough to send James Earl Ray into a frenzy of passionate hate.

The FBI put Ray at the top of its Ten Most Wanted Fugitives list, something his file revealed was the assassin's longstanding personal ambition.

As every police agency in the country prioritised the manhunt for James Earl Ray, information began to flow across James Doherty's desk. Ray was identified by sales staff at Aeromarine Supply in Birmingham, Alabama, as the purchaser of the murder weapon on 30 March 1968, under the alias Harvey Lowmeyer. He was also identified as the man who rented a room at Bessie Brewer's rooming house under the alias John Willard.

But then, much to Doherty's frustration, the trail went cold. There were no more reported sightings until a clerk at the Atlanta Greyhound terminal remembered selling a ticket to a man resembling Ray on 6 April. Ticket sale receipts revealed a number of possible destinations, but Doherty had a feeling that James Earl Ray would try to leave the country.

He called to request an urgent meeting with Arthur Simpson and was told to attend the director's office. Putting on his jacket and straightening his tie, Doherty took the elevator to the fifth floor and was ushered into J Edgar Hoover's suite.

'Doherty,' Hoover proclaimed with his trademark crooked grin. 'I hear you've been working around the clock on the King assassination. What do you have for me?'

'Nothing more than a theory, sir.'

'Well, a good theory is better than no theory at all,' replied Hoover. 'So out with it.'

'Well, sir, we've traced Ray to the bus station in Atlanta, which makes sense because that's where he dumped the white Mustang. One of the clerks thinks he recognises Ray's mugshot, but doesn't remember the destination of the ticket he sold. But if I had just committed the highest profile murder in the world, what would I be doing?'

'Well?' prompted Hoover.

'I'd be trying to get out of the country,' volunteered Doherty.

Doherty nodded. 'Exactly, sir. And that means either Canada or Mexico.'

'Any idea which?' asked Hoover.

Doherty shrugged. 'I'd choose Mexico, but then I'm not a fanatical racist who thinks all brown people are inferior.'

'One would hope not,' joked Hoover.

Doherty was able to summon a tired smile, just. 'So, I think he's in Canada.'

Hoover nodded. 'I'll inform the president and talk to Malcolm Lindsay at the Royal Canadian Mounted Police. Now, Doherty, I want you to go home. You look as though you're about to keel over.'

'But sir,' Doherty protested, falling silent before the stern gaze of the FBI director.

'You've been working non-stop since we called you at home three weeks ago. You've been doing an outstanding job, but I want you to go home, rest and recharge. See your wife … Arlene, isn't it?' Hoover asked with a sly glance at his offsider, Clyde Tolson, who nodded.

Doherty assumed Tolson had briefed Hoover on his personal details just before the meeting. 'Yes, sir.'

'So, I'm ordering you to take a week off,' said Hoover. 'When you're back, report directly to me. By the way, what do you think of counterespionage?'

Doherty did a double take in spite of his fatigue. 'Counterespionage? Well, sir, I know the Russians are a real threat.'

'Indeed they are,' replied Hoover, rising to his feet in an implicit sign of dismissal. 'And when you're back on deck I'll be putting you in a position to do something about it.'

'Thank you, sir.' Doherty left and returned to his desk where he picked up the phone and dialled home.

'Honey, I have a week off, but if I get behind the wheel, I'm afraid I'll run into a tree. Can you pick me up?'

Forty minutes later he was waiting at the corner of 9th and Pennsylvania Avenue as Arlene pulled up the family Chrysler. He sighed with relief as he slid into the front passenger seat and gave his wife a tired kiss.

James Doherty spent the first ten hours of his leave in deep, restful sleep. The remainder of that week he spent with his wife and children, rested and tried to avoid the television.

Reporting back to Director Hoover, Doherty found himself assigned to supervise a counterintelligence investigation into espionage being conducted out of the Russian Embassy in Washington. With twenty-five agents and analysts working twenty-four hours a day under his direction, he had little time to ponder the progress, or lack thereof, on the investigation into the assassination of Dr King.

Therefore, James Doherty was something of an onlooker when news broke on 8 June 1968 that James Earl Ray had been arrested in Great Britain. However, he did take the time to read the FBI's internal investigation report.

When he read that Ray travelled by bus from Atlanta to Detroit, Doherty was gratified his hunch had been right. Ray had crossed the border into Canada on 6 April and managed to obtain a Canadian passport under the name of Ramon George Sneyd. Ray Sneyd then flew to London on 6 May, swapping a return ticket to Canada for a flight to Lisbon. He arrived in Portugal on 7 May, hoping to find passage on a boat to Africa. Ray's intended destination was white supremacist Rhodesia, which had no extradition agreement with the United States.

But James Earl Ray missed the boat—both literally and figuratively. Faced with dwindling funds, he returned to London on 17 May where he embarked on an abortive robbery spree. By the beginning of June, Scotland Yard investigators connected the dots between Ray and Sneyd, and both names were put on the airport 'Passport Watch List'. When Ray tried to buy a ticket to Brussels at London's Heathrow Airport on 8 June, he was arrested with two Canadian passports and a loaded gun in his possession.

In addition to his other responsibilities, James Doherty kept abreast of the progress of the case against James Earl Ray, both from the press and internal FBI reports.

Ray was extradited to the United States and on 19 July 1968 returned at the scene of his crime—Memphis, Tennessee—this time in shackles.

His court-appointed lawyers found James Earl Ray to be a difficult client. But after firing his first attorney, a lawyer by the name of Percy Foreman, managed to convince Ray that his case was doomed to failure if it went to trial.

On 10 March 1969, James Earl Ray accepted a plea deal in which he would avoid the death penalty in favour of a ninety-nine-year term of imprisonment at the Brushy Mountain State Penitentiary.

'I hope he rots there,' spat Debra Doherty as the family watched the evening news report of the James Earl Ray plea agreement.

'So do I,' proclaimed Arlene Doherty, earning an arched brow of surprise from James.

'It seems we're all in agreement, then,' he said. 'I suggest we make a formal family decision never to mention that man's name again. Agreed?'

Arlene and the twins nodded.

From that moment, James Earl Ray was consigned to the dustbin of the Doherty family consciousness.

END NOTE

The sense of national shock and horror over the assassination of Dr Martin Luther King, Jr, resonated throughout the United States.

For some, his death confirmed their belief that nonviolent methods would never be enough to improve the lot of African Americans.

Amid a wave of national grief and urban riots, President Lyndon B Johnson urged Americans to 'reject the blind violence' that had killed Dr King, whom he called the 'apostle of nonviolence'. He appealed to Congress to pass the civil rights legislation as a fitting legacy to Dr King and his life's work.

On 11 April, President Johnson signed the Fair Housing Act—civil rights legislation that prohibited discrimination on race, religion, national origin or gender in the sale, rental and financing of housing. The wave of violence that erupted in the wake of the assassination of Dr King eventually subsided after police around the country were reinforced by 58,000 United States national guard and army troops.

The assassination was a horrific event in a year that became noted for turbulence and discord. On 30 January 1968, the Vietcong and North Vietnamese opened their famous Tet Offensive, which shattered public confidence in the prospects of an American victory. Images of the United States embassy in Saigon under siege eviscerated the official Pentagon narrative that the war effort was going well. Rising public opposition to the war eventually led President Johnson to withdraw his bid for re-election to a second term. And on 6 June 1968, Democratic presidential candidate Robert Kennedy—brother of John F Kennedy—was murdered by Palestinian assassin, Sirhan.

Dr King's opposition to the Vietnam War had been building steadily since 1965. At first, he had been reluctant to criticise the war because President Johnson provided essential support for the passage of the *Civil Rights Act of 1964* and the *Voting Rights Act of 1965*.

However, as time passed, Dr King's anti-war stance hardened

and he became more outspoken in his criticism of what he described as American militarism and imperialism. His turn to the political left was also reflected in his growing critique of capitalism, which he began to assail as the source of both economic and racial inequality.

Many in the American political establishment came to view Dr King as a dangerous radical. Yet in the eyes of some younger African American activists, he wasn't nearly radical enough.

By the late 1960s, Dr King's earlier civil rights triumphs in Montgomery, Birmingham, and Selma, Alabama, were little more than faded memories to many younger African Americans. Black Nationalist leader Malcolm X described Dr King's strategy of non-violence as 'criminal'. Firebrands like Stokely Carmichael, who later Africanised his name to Kwame Ture, argued for a more confrontational approach. As civil rights historian David J Garrow tells it, at one face-to-face meeting, Carmichael sought to 'force' Dr King to 'take a stand for Black Power'.

Some scholars argue that Dr King's shift to the political left had been the result of pressure from younger and more radical black activists. Be that as it may, in November 1967, King's focus on economic inequality had led him and his Southern Christian Leadership Conference to organise a Poor People's Campaign that culminated in a massive March on Washington DC on 28 August 1968.

Meanwhile, Richard Nixon won the Republican nomination and, ultimately, the presidency on a platform of supporting a 'silent majority' of Americans who opposed radical social change and supported the war. But Nixon's Watergate skulduggery forced him from office six years later, and he became the only American president ever to resign in disgrace.

While Nixon and the silent majority may have won a temporary tactical victory in 1968, it can be argued that the legacy of Martin Luther King, Jr, will live on forever.

Martin Luther King, Jr, at a press conference
World Telegram & Sun photo by Walter Albertin, 8 June 1964

8. POOR PEOPLE'S CAMPAIGN, WASHINGTON 1968

MAY 1968

I suppose it would be fair to describe me as a 'red diaper baby'—one of those kids born to Lower East Side parents whose Marxist devotion remained undiminished by Stalin's purges or even the Molotov–Ribbentrop Pact. The ultimate triumph of the proletariat through class conflict was an article of faith in our household. To challenge any facet of dialectical materialism would have been heresy of the first order.

It will, therefore, come as no surprise to the reader that I cut my political teeth in the Young Communist League, now rebadged under the name 'American Youth for Democracy'. By the time I matriculated from Swarthmore College, I was a seasoned polemicist, well-versed in the intricacies of Marxist economic, social and political theory.

My crisis of conscience came a few months after the events I'm about to describe. The sight of Soviet tanks bulldozing their way through barricades in the streets of Prague caused me to question everything I'd been taught. I felt, and still feel, deep concern about the social, racial and economic inequities that are the inevitable by-product of American capitalism. But after the brutal suppression of Czech pro-democracy demonstrators in August 1968, I could no longer accept my parents' brand of blind subservience to whatever line emanated from the Kremlin.

My personal transition from Marxist true believer to social democrat sceptic in the wake of the Soviet invasion of Czechoslovakia is a matter for another time. It is, however, relevant to note that when I first began to work on behalf of the Poor People's Campaign or PPC in May 1968, I had yet to undergo this metamorphosis.

The founder of the PPC, the martyred Martin Luther King, Jr, had expressed his principled opposition to communism, describing it as a system 'that reduces men to a cog in the wheel of the state'. Not that this emphatic denunciation stopped the FBI from wild rumour-mongering about a mythical Kremlin connection in order to discredit Dr King and his movement.

Therefore, for reasons of philosophy, as well as pragmatism, the Reverend Ralph Abernathy, who succeeded Martin Luther King, Jr, to the leadership of the PPC, rebuffed all overtures of support from radical elements such as the Communist Party USA and the Black Panthers. With this in mind, I kept my Marxist sentiments to myself. While there's probably a file with my name on it somewhere in the bowels of the FBI archives, I suppose I was never important enough for J Edgar Hoover to pay me much attention. Or perhaps his sub rosa surveillance state wasn't that efficient after all.

At the time, I was a twenty-four-year-old graduate student in philosophy at the University of Virginia, who had taken a leave of absence after the assassination of Martin Luther King, Jr, that April. I felt the best way to honour Dr King's memory was to help bring to fruition his final project—the Poor People's Campaign.

The PPC was conceived by Dr King as a means of pressuring decision-makers in Washington to heed the concerns of the USA's poor. From its inception, the movement was designed to transcend race and ethnicity. It expressed equal concern about the fates of impoverished Appalachian whites, Southern sharecroppers, nomadic Mexican-American farm workers and destitute inner-city blacks. Dr King believed that the struggle against institutional poverty was a cause that could, and should, unite people of all races, backgrounds and creeds.

Dr King had laid out the goals of the PPC at a press conference in February 1968. They included an annual government expenditure of US$3 billion in anti-poverty programs, which would be equivalent to US$22.5 billion in 2021, a government-guaranteed minimum income, and construction of 500,000 units of public housing each year.

While his ideals were lofty, Dr King was enough of a pragmatist to realise that such an ambitious social welfare program would be dead-on-arrival in Washington, circa 1968. He understood the only way to overcome resolute opposition from the American political establishment would be through the exertion of political pressure.

So, Dr King designed the PPC to exploit the lessons learned over fifteen years of civil rights activism. Peaceful protests against social and economic injustice would seize the moral high ground, thereby attracting sympathetic coverage in the media. Non-violent acts of civil disobedience would be tailored to embarrass the political powers that be. If that embarrassment triggered an overreaction by the authorities, all the better. A brutal police response would shift the moral centre of gravity even farther in the protesters' favour.

There might be those who are inclined to question whether this strategy of expediency was morally justified. While I entertained similar doubts when I first joined the PPC, I ultimately concluded that the answer was 'yes'.

Bear in mind that we were making social and economic demands that were vast in scope. It would be naïve to think resistance to the PPC platform could be overcome easily. Dr King understood that only by ratcheting up political pressure would it become more painful for Congress to retain the status quo than to change it, so, that's what we set out to do.

A multi-ethnic group of prominent leaders, dubbed the 'Committee of 100', began a political lobbying campaign in Washington's corridors of power. It was this group that crystallised the five formal demands of the PPC: a meaningful job at a living wage, a secure and adequate income for those unable to work, access to land for economic uses, access to capital for the poor, and empowering the political participation of 'ordinary people'.

The most colourful contingent travelling to Washington for the Poor People's Campaign was the mule train from Marks, Mississippi. Just a few days before his assassination, Dr King spoke at Washington DC's National Cathedral about the pervasive poverty he encountered during a trip through the township of Marks. He described throngs of black children walking barefoot because their sharecropping families couldn't afford to buy shoes. He thought the impoverished Mississippi Delta town would serve as the perfect exemplar for a political campaign to highlight the economic injustice faced by America's poor.

My first stop was Atlanta, where I attended a mandatory training session for PPC volunteer staff in the meeting hall at Ebenezer Baptist Church. After signing a pledge to observe the principles of non-violence, I was then dispatched to Marks with the title of 'marshal', a fancy name for an organiser and recruiter. There was no prospect of pay. I lived off savings and occasional Western Union wire transfers from my parents while racking up hundreds of miles in my 1962 VW Beetle travelling through the Mississippi Delta trying to enlist people in the campaign.

As a born-and-bred New Yorker, I was shocked by the semi-feudal economic system that dominated, not thirteenth-century France nor nineteenth-century Russia, but this rural region of twentieth-century America. The Mississippi Delta was dominated by large plantations run under the sharecropping system, where farmers—invariably black—lived as tenants on the property owned by large landholders—invariably white. These tenant farmers paid their rents with a portion of their harvested crop, making do with what little was left.

Sharecropping was a recipe for perpetual poverty, the closest thing to slavery you could find in a country where servitude had been outlawed a century earlier by constitutional amendment. Most heartbreaking was the fate of children, who were forced to labour in the fields rather than acquire the education that would enable them to have a better life. The entire system was a disgraceful relic of an old South that I was doing my small part to help end.

By early May, I'd recruited over fifty people from Marks and the surrounding areas willing to journey by mule-drawn wagons to Washington. The Marks, Mississippi, mule train set out on 13 May 1968 with a convoy of fifteen covered wagons emblazoned with slogans like, 'Feed the Poor' and 'Which is better? Send man to the Moon, or feed him on Earth?' I left my trusty VW in the care of the elders of the Eudora African Methodist Episcopal Zion

Church, where Martin Luther King, Jr, had spoken a few months before his assassination, and took my place on the front seat of the lead wagon.

Travelling at around twenty-five miles per day, we headed for Atlanta, sleeping under the stars or, when it rained, beneath our wagons. A confirmed city boy, I realised that my personal discomfort at these rudimentary living arrangements added much to the amusement of my fellows in the mule train who had been toughened by hard, outdoor lives labouring in the fields. Their general attitude towards me was one-third amusement, one-third compassion and one-third appreciation for sharing their cause.

The sight of our convoy plodding through Mississippi and Alabama drew substantial public attention, much of it negative. On occasion, passing cars filled with whites of the redneck variety pelted us with invective and projectiles, usually food or soda bottles that missed. I took to ostentatiously focusing my Kodak camera, which seemed to deter them from anything more serious.

As we passed along the byways of the deep South, we also came upon blacks who would smile as they gazed upon the mule train with hope-filled eyes. With each such encounter, my spirits would lift and my determination to persevere would strengthen. The shared rigours of the road also bridged the vast gulf in education and economic background between me and the others on the mule train. Our common cause, and the adversity we experienced, transformed us into brothers and sisters. Within the space of a few days, I felt as though these were people I had known my entire life.

On 25 May we reached Atlanta, loading our wagons on flatcars and our mules on freight carriages. The Marks mule train then spent the next two days travelling by rail to Alexandria, Virginia, where we unloaded and were joined by a larger crowd of PPC participants for our final entry into Washington. In addition to my Mississippi sharecropping fellow-travellers, I encountered all kinds of people—white, middle-class college students from the Midwest, itinerant farm workers from faraway California, and manual labourers from inner-city Baltimore, all united by their common distress about the economic inequity plaguing America.

We crossed the Potomac on the Arlington Memorial Bridge to the glare of popping flashbulbs from a pack of press photographers, and turned right towards a point south of the Reflecting Pool where the Korean War Memorial stands today. The area was a hive of activity. People were unloading timber boards and lengths of canvas from two dozen trucks. Others were using the materials to erect tents in neat rows that resembled a military encampment.

As I clambered down from the seat of my wagon, I felt a tap on my shoulder and looked around to see a face I recognised from our Atlanta training session.

'It's Reverend Abernathy. He's calling you.'

I looked in the direction they indicated and saw that the icon of the civil rights movement was beckoning for me to join him.

'Weber, isn't it?' smiled Abernathy, in his Alabama drawl. 'I've heard good things about you.'

'Thank you, sir,' I replied. 'Just doing what I can.'

Abernathy smiled. 'Well, thank you,' replied Abernathy.

'You're a graduate student, I've been told.'

'Yes, sir,' I replied. 'PhD program in philosophy at UVA.'

Abernathy nodded. 'That's good. We always need people who can organise and lead. Otherwise, this all could turn into a mess.'

'I'm happy to do whatever I can to help,' I replied.

'Well, let's get to it. I'm turning you over to the none-too-tender mercies of Ken Jadin,' said Abernathy, nodding his head to indicate a bespectacled young white man standing a few feet away. 'Ken is the architect who designed what we're going to call Resurrection City.'

Abernathy placed his hand on my shoulder in an avuncular gesture. 'He's all yours, Ken.'

'Hi,' said Jadin as we shook hands. 'So, how handy are you with a hammer?'

'Not great,' I said, 'I'm a philosopher in training.'

Jadin laughed. 'Then I guess we should consider this to be a bit of OJT training.'

My brow furrowed.

'OJT … on-the-job training,' he explained.

'Ah. Sorry for being obtuse. What about you?'

'Me?' Jardin shrugged. 'Bachelor of Architecture from the University of Oklahoma and a couple of masters from Penn.'

'Isn't that where Frank Lloyd Wright studied?' I asked. 'Oklahoma, I mean.'

'Yup,' nodded Jardin. 'That's why I went there. But time's awastin', so let's get down to business.'

Jardin pointed towards the piles of lumber and canvas that were growing by the minute. 'The UAW— United Auto Workers to you and me—and some other friends have been very generous. As you can see, we're using that money to build a tent city on the mall at the foot of the Lincoln Memorial.'

I nodded. 'The symbolism is powerful.'

'That's the idea,' Jardin confirmed. 'Especially in light of the fact that almost exactly five years ago Dr King delivered his "I have a dream" speech right there.'

I nodded. 'And don't forget the legacy of the Bonus Army.'

Jardin sighed. 'I hope we don't end the same way,' he said,

referring to the violent dispersal of an encampment of army veterans and their wives and children during the Great Depression who had come to Washington seeking bonus payment for their war service.

Jardin opened a shoulder bag and unfolded an architectural blueprint. 'As you can see, the shelter design is pretty simple. A wooden frame of two-by-four erected on top of a framed wooden floor and then covered by canvas. It's summer, so we won't have a problem with cold.'

'I should warn you that giving me a hammer constitutes a menace to anyone within a five-foot radius,' I told him.

Jardin laughed. 'Then you can be my dogsbody. Every great leader of men needs a dogsbody.'

'Sounds good to me,' I said with a sardonic grin.

So, I became Ken Jardin's gopher. I ran errands and conveyed instructions as Resurrection City took shape. One of the high points came when I was asked to give Eunice Kennedy Shriver—sister of the assassinated JFK—a guided tour. I was even more starstruck when she rolled up her sleeves and got to work with hammer and saw, helping to build shelters. Much to my chagrin, it turned out that even a female, Massachusetts blue-blood was more of a carpenter than I was. Eunice later left Washington after her brother Robert Kennedy was murdered in Los Angeles by a Palestinian assassin on 6 June. Needless to say, we were all crushed by the brutal murder of this second scion of that tragedy-plagued family.

By the end of May there were around three hundred tents along the mall housing roughly ten times that number of protesters. Numbers of loudspeakers were erected atop telephone poles, and the encampment echoed with news bulletins, meeting announcements and even a few long-distance telephone calls of support. There were several medical tents manned by volunteer doctors and nurses, as well as a kitchen where volunteer cooks prepared steaming vats of stew and beans. Our food and pharmaceuticals came from donations. But aspirin and penicillin were not the only drugs present in the encampment—more about the seamier side of Resurrection City later.

Each morning, weather permitting, we would assemble in a central square where our marching orders for the day were delivered, either by Reverend Abernathy or his lieutenants, Hosea Williams and Jesse Jackson, Jr, who had been appointed joint managers of Resurrection City, which was even given its own postcode of 20013.

I found Williams to be an impressive man, a combat veteran who was wounded fighting in General George Patton's Third Army. He finished high school after the war and went on to earn bachelor and master's degrees in chemistry. He then studied for ordination as a Methodist minister from Atlanta University, and joined Dr King's Southern Christian Leadership Conference, rising to the position of field director. Speaking in a deep Alabama drawl, Hosea Williams exuded a sense of gravitas that inspired confidence in people. At least it did with me.

By contrast, Jesse Jackson struck me as someone who was motivated by an element of self-interest. He became known around the encampment as a media hound. People would joke that the most dangerous place in Resurrection City is anywhere between Jesse Jackson and a TV camera.

One of the more disturbing stories making the rounds involved Jesse Jackson's self-aggrandising behaviour in the aftermath of Martin Luther King, Jr's assassination. Jackson was present at the

Lorraine Motel in Memphis on 4 April 1968, working as a junior aide to Dr King when the assassin's fatal bullet was fired. Claiming that he'd fallen ill, Jackson made haste and flew home to Chicago, where he appeared the following morning on the *Today* show still wearing the shirt he claimed was stained with Dr King's blood. Encampment rumour had it that Hosea Williams despised Jesse Jackson as a result of this incident, but the two deputy leaders of Resurrection City maintained a surface pretence of comity throughout the Poor People's Campaign.

Our modus operandi was simple. Each day the protesters would assemble at the headquarters of a different federal government agency to demand action on the five-point plan of the PPC. The departments of Labor, the Treasury, Housing and Urban Development were just a few of the offices where protests occurred.

On some occasions, demonstrations were mounted to reflect the partisan concerns of a single group within the PPC coalition. Then, on 29 May, I followed Dakota Sioux chief, George Crow Flies High, to the front steps of the Supreme Court to protest against a judicial ruling that enabled state governments to restrict Native American traditional fishing rights. Delegations from the PPC also met with supportive members of Congress. Invariably, they were liberal Democrats. Invariably, they were powerless to deliver anything other than a sympathetic ear.

At the end of May, I was assigned to liaise with another hero of civil rights history, Bayard Rustin, who played a major role in the 1963 March on Washington where Martin Luther King, Jr, delivered his 'I have a dream' speech. The hope was to recreate the energy and political power of the March on Washington by hosting a massive rally at the same location—the Lincoln Memorial.

Solidarity Day, as the event was to be called, was scheduled for 8 June. However, as we began to spread the word through our nationwide network of civil rights and allied organisations, I had a ringside seat to disagreements over strategy that erupted into outright enmity between Abernathy and Rustin.

Rustin was insistent that Solidarity Day maintain a singular orientation on social and economic issues, employment, racial discrimination in housing and health care. But Abernathy, mindful of the broad range of groups that made up the PPC coalition, sought to adopt a broader suite of topics that included non-economic issues such as the Vietnam War. The arguments over strategic focus grew louder and more bitter until, on 8 June, Rustin announced his withdrawal from the PPC.

Solidarity Day was ultimately scheduled for 19 June, a date long celebrated by blacks as 'Juneteenth,' the day commemorating the official demise of slavery in 1865. In some respects, Solidarity Day was a great success, with Martin Luther King, Jr's widow, Coretta Scott King, delivering the keynote address to an estimated audience of fifty thousand people. The crowds attending Solidarity Day temporarily distracted from the problems that were festering beneath the surface of Resurrection City. As the people dispersed, these problems continued to intensify—illness, poverty, racial conflict, organisational problems ... the list grew and grew.

Days passed into weeks without tangible political results, and morale within the encampment began to ebb. A series of summer storms turned the area into a muddy morass. While some Resurrection City residents worked hard to meet the logistical needs of the community, others descended into idleness. This growing distinction between lifters and leaners bred ill-will and resentment, which at times erupted into violence. Drug use became overt and complaints about property crime proliferated. My camera and sleeping-bag were stolen, never to be recovered.

Morale worsened further when camp residents discovered that Ralph Abernathy had taken up residence in a hotel, rather than endure the living conditions in Resurrection City. Not only did this shatter my illusions about one of the civil rights movement's greatest icons, but it taught me an enduring lesson about leadership. Never during my subsequent career did I ask my subordinates to do something I was not prepared to do myself. If they worked late, so would I. Leadership by personal example became a fundamental pillar of my personal philosophy.

Then we learned that most of the Chicano contingent had taken up residence at an alternative school some two and a half miles away in the Southwest Waterfront neighbourhood of Washington. While some activists tried to spin this as the triumphant creation of a multicultural coalition of Hispanics, poor Appalachian whites and blacks, the rest of us who remained mired in the mud of Resurrection City viewed it as another betrayal.

People began to abandon the encampment, at first in dribs and drabs, then a flood of departures. I left before the camping permit from the National Park Service expired at midnight on 23 June and the Washington Metropolitan Police moved in without delay. The next morning—24 June 1968—a phalanx of a thousand police officers moved through Resurrection City, pushing out the remaining residents who, by that time, numbered only about five hundred.

So, as it turned out, my forebodings about a repeat of the Bonus Army incident during the Great Depression proved prescient. The only difference was that the US Army expelled people in 1932, while in 1968 it was the Washington DC police. And, fortunately, nobody was shot.

As for me, I heard about the demise of Resurrection City on the radio while driving my Beetle from Marks, Mississippi, back to my apartment in Charlottesville, Virginia. Along the way, I thought long and hard about my future. Did I really want to pursue an academic career in an esoteric field like philosophy? By the end of my journey, I didn't think so.

But I stuck out my PhD program, writing a dissertation on the ethics of non-violent protest in democracy. After receiving my doctorate, I applied for a job as a foreign service officer at the US Agency for International Development in hopes of devoting my life to deeds rather than thoughts.

I was pleasantly surprised that my youthful dalliance with Marxism didn't disqualify me from government service. Perhaps a reformed sinner is more highly regarded than someone who has never sinned in the first place. Or maybe the success of my application to join USAID is a validation of my doubts about the efficiency of the FBI. In any event, it is now sixteen years later, and I write these words from Rome where I've been seconded by USAID to the headquarters of the World Food Program.

I'd like to think that my decade-and-a-half of experience in the international aid business might afford me some particular insight into the Poor People's Campaign of 1968. It is self-evident that even at the height of the swinging 60s, the PPC's agenda was several bridges too far for the mainstream of the American people. With Ronald Reagan on track to win a second term at this year's presidential election, it could be rightly said that the PPC's agenda is still too progressive, and perhaps more so.

For the sake of complete honesty, I must confess that the real catalyst for this account was the implosion of Jesse Jackson's presidential primary bid over a series of anti-Semitic remarks he made to a *Washington Post* reporter. While bigotry in all its forms is a noxious blight on humanity, I can't deny a frisson of schadenfreude over how the 'Hymietown' controversy validated my assessment of Jackson's character.

9. THE 1968 DEMOCRATIC NATIONAL CONVENTION

AUGUST 1968

'You wanted to see me?' Young Andrew Lamb tried to hide any outward sign of trepidation. After only six weeks on the job at *The San Francisco Independent*, a summons to the office of the editor could be good or it could be bad.

Ramsey Thomas looked up from the pile of papers strewn across his desk.

'Ah, Lamb ... yes. Simpson was assigned to cover the Democratic National Convention in Chicago, but he ended up in the emergency room with abdominal pain. Turns out he has goddamned appendicitis. So, pack your bags. You're booked on the 9 am to O'Hare tomorrow morning. Clara in HR has your tickets, hotel reservations and walking-around money.'

'Ah ... yes. Thank you,' stuttered Andrew.

'There's trouble brewing and I want you to be all over it. Thousands of anti-war activists are flowing into Chicago and there are already demonstrations in the streets. I can't see the Daley machine turning a blind eye to that sort of thing. It all smells like a riot brewing to me.'

'But ... I'm not a political reporter,' Andrew protested. 'I've been on the obit desk.'

'Well, you are now.' Thomas smiled. 'Congratulations on your promotion. You won't be at the convention itself. That's Grierson's job. Instead, I want you covering those protests like a blanket. Are you clear about that?'

'Yes, sir.'

Thomas responded with the regal nod of someone in a position of absolute authority. 'Remember, Lamb, if you mess this up, you'll be a lamb to the slaughter. Your career will be as dead as the people you've been writing obituaries about.'

'Right,' gulped Andrew.

'And one more thing. Remember who we are. *The San Francisco Independent* was established as an alternative to the *Chronicle* and *Examiner*. We make no bones about our progressive editorial world view. That's what our readers want and that's what I expect you to deliver. None of this objective journalism nonsense. I want you to slay all the establishment sacred cows you can find. Do you understand what I'm saying?'

'Y-yes, sir.'

'Then, good luck. Go get 'em, tiger.'

Andrew scooted out of his editor's office and proceeded to HR, where he picked up his tickets, hotel reservation and expense money. The next stop was the Doe Memorial Library at UC Berkeley to brush up on the politics surrounding the Democratic National Convention he'd been assigned to cover. On the way he found a phone box and called an old classmate, Karen King, who was not only politically astute, but also politically active. She was surprised to hear from him, but when he explained what he needed, she was happy to talk.

'Well, the calls have gone out to Yippies, hippies and any other protesters to attend demos at the Democratic National Convention,' Karen told him. 'MOBE—the National Mobilisation Committee to End the War in Vietnam,' she added for his benefit, '... and Yippies met up to coordinate joint protest action in Chicago. The two groups have different agendas and different modes of activism. MOBE apparently got a permit for their protests, while the Yippies are mainly on about their counterculture values. But both groups hate the Democrats and Hubert Humphrey isn't the most inspiring individual,' she concluded dryly.

Andrew was scrawling in his notebook, the phone tucked between shoulder and ear. 'So, MOBE ...?' he began.

'MOBE's National Coordinator is Rennie Davis. He's vowed to flood Chicago with thousands of anti-war protesters. And Abbie Hoffman and Jerry Rubin are planning a festival of some kind—youth, music, theatre, that kind of thing,' she sounded slightly scornful.

'And they are ...'

'Yippies. They demand the politics of ecstasy, whatever that means.' Karen was clearly not a fan. 'But they issued a statement saying they wouldn't be stopped by threats from LBJ, or Mayor Daley or J Edgar Freako.'

'Thanks, Karen,' Andrew said, scribbling furiously. 'Can I call you if I have any other questions?'

'Sure, happy to help,' she said, 'and when you get back, you owe me a drink, okay?'

'Sure,' Andrew stuttered, 'that'd be great.'

As he ploughed through back issues of *Time* and *Newsweek*, Andrew took a moment to ponder how he had stumbled into such an opportunity a mere two months after graduating with a Bachelor of Arts degree from UC Berkeley.

This turn of events was all the more serendipitous because politics had never been his passion, a fact Karen understood. Yes, the free-speech movement was roiling across the Berkeley campus during his freshman year of college, but his primary focus at the time was snagging a sports column in the student newspaper, the *Daily Californian*. Growing up in La Jolla, his role model was not Walter Cronkite, but *San Diego Union* sportswriter, Jack Murphy. When it came to dream jobs, a newsbeat covering his beloved San Diego Chargers topped the list, but the obits desk at *The San Francisco Independent* was the only Bay Area job he could find after graduation. He grabbed it with both hands.

Of course, he wasn't completely oblivious to the convulsions that had been shaking the social fabric of the United States over the past few years. They were far too big and destructive for any sentient person to miss. He was well aware of the festering anti-Vietnam War movement. He saw TV footage of race riots ravaging Detroit, Newark, Los Angeles and other American cities. He was horrified by the assassinations of Martin Luther King, Jr, in April and Robert Kennedy in June.

But as he sat in the library, delving into the gory political details of the past few years, Andrew Lamb had something of a personal revelation. For the first time it occurred to him that perhaps his lack of interest in politics and countervailing obsession with sports were a subconscious escape mechanism. While reading about the Yippies—activists of the Youth International Party (YIP)—he had a premonition that he was about to run face-first into real-world ugliness.

After his three-hour refresher course on recent current affairs,

Andrew went home to pack, throwing an extra pair of jeans, T-shirts, a sweater, underwear and socks into an overnight bag. A Leica M2 with six rolls of extra film, three spiral notebooks and half-a-dozen ballpoint pens went into a canvas satchel with a leather shoulder strap. The following morning, he was at San Francisco International Airport boarding a TWA flight to Chicago O'Hare.

After take-off, Andrew lifted a copy of the *Chicago Tribune* from his satchel. The lead story was the looming Democratic National Convention.

Landing in Chicago, Andrew snagged a taxicab and went straight to the Hilton Chicago on Michigan Avenue, grateful that Ramsey Thomas was generous enough to put him up in comfort. He unpacked, showered and walked downstairs for a drink. It had been a long flight and he decided to have an early night.

After breakfast the next morning, Andrew stepped onto the street and saw thousands of anti-war protesters and counterculture activists flowing into the city. He'd read Mayor Richard Daley's determination to promote his city to the world and pledge never to allow thousands of long-haired protesters to disrupt his city's role as host of the DNC.

Slinging his satchel over one shoulder, Andrew made his way across Michigan Avenue into Grant Park, which was teeming with the various tribes of the protest movement. There were Yippies with unkempt hair and tie-dyed T-shirts alongside beret-wearing Black Panthers. Representatives of the late Martin Luther King, Jr's Southern Christian Leadership Conference in their suits and ties conferred with grim-faced MOBE anti-war activists.

As he mingled, Andrew suddenly heard angry shouts from a crowd gathered around a telephone pole.

'What's going on?' he asked a young woman with long, brown braids and a flowing, full-length skirt.

'The fucking city won't allow us to set up camp, that's what. See for yourself,' she fumed, pointing towards a notice affixed to the pole with industrial staples.

Andrew pushed through the crowd until he could read it.

> As of 11 pm Saturday 24 August 1968, a curfew will be in force along the Lake Michigan foreshore in Lincoln, Millennium and Grant parks. Camping or overnight stays in these areas is prohibited.
>
> Signed, David Stahl, City Administrator

'What are you going to do?' Andrew asked the young man standing next to him.

'I hear the Yippies are trying to get an emergency court order,' the man snorted, 'but there's no way any Chicago judge will have the balls to go up against the Daley machine. Who are you, man?'

'I'm Andrew Lamb from *The San Francisco Independent*. We're a paper out in the Bay Area. And what's your name?'

'Cool,' replied the Yippie in a tone of respect. 'I'm Sam Tripplin from Charlottesville, Virginia.'

'Go Cavaliers,' grinned Andrew.

'Wah-hoo-wa!' Tripplin shouted the chant of University of Virginia football fans after every touchdown their team scored.

'So again,' pressed Andrew, 'what are you going to do?'

Tripplin shrugged. 'People power, man. Even Richard fuckin' Daley can't stand against the people's will.'

'T-r-i-p-l-i-n?' queried Andrew, scribbling on his notepad.

'Two p's,' grinned Tripplin. 'Common mistake.'

'Thanks a lot,' replied Andrew. 'I'm going to keep moving.'

'Don't forget this,' said Tripplin, tearing the broadside from the telephone pole. It'll look good on the front page of your paper.'

'Thanks, man.' Andrew folded the flyer and placed it in his satchel.

Andrew spent the rest of the day wandering through Grant and Millennial parks, talking to Panthers, hippies and other groups of protesters. Most outrage focused on the police shooting a few days earlier of a young man named Dean Johnson, rather than the mayor's curfew order. That afternoon, news swept through the crowd that a federal district judge denied the request for an injunction against the curfew. As night fell on Saturday, the rumour spread that thousands of Illinois national guardsmen were being deployed to Chicago.

Yet Andrew remained, interviewing members of the crowd and waiting for something to happen, but nothing did, at least not that night. A climax of sorts came at 10.45 pm when a Chicago police lieutenant announced through a bullhorn turned up to maximum volume, 'Grant Park will close to the public in fifteen minutes. Anyone found within the park after that time will be subject to arrest.'

Then Andrew was surprised to see Beat Generation poet, Allen Ginsburg, materialise from among the crowd. Andrew had been an admirer of Ginsburg's writing since reading *Howl* in his sophomore year at Berkeley, and had read it and re-read it many times since. Now he watched, a tad starstruck, as Ginsburg led a cavalcade of protesters in the Vedic meditative chant 'om' as they marched out of Grant Park. Thrilled at this close encounter with one of his literary idols, Andrew decided to call it a night.

After a sound six and a half hours of sleep, Andrew arose that

Sunday morning and drank a quick cup of coffee before crossing into Grant Park to see what he could see. The rumour mill when he arrived told him that protest leaders had been meeting to discuss whether Mayor Daley's park curfew should be respected. As the story went, there was disagreement over tactics between Yippie founders, Jerry Rubin and Abbie Hoffman, with Hoffman joining Rennie David and Tom Hyden to argue for non-violent resistance to the curfew order.

The weather was beautiful, the best type of late-summer Michigan day with clear skies and a temperature in the mid-seventies. Andrew wandered through Lincoln Park, collecting anecdotes that would add colour to the feature article he would soon begin writing. What he found was a veritable human-interest kaleidoscope.

He photographed people swaying in trance-like fashion to the tempo of beating drums. Other groups were singing Dylan and Baez songs to the accompaniment of ubiquitous guitars. Couples were making out on the grass, heedless of the fact they were in full public view. Down by the lagoon, a group of hippies was distributing flowers while declaiming poetry. The smell of marijuana was everywhere and Andrew gained the distinct impression that it was far from the only illicit drug in circulation. Some of what Andrew encountered struck him as hilarious, such as the obviously stoned hippie yelling, 'Did you ever make love to a tree?'

The morning passed without major incident, but tensions began to rise in the early afternoon when a group of protesters marched through Chicago's famous Loop district chanting anti-war slogans. Andrew watched as a brief confrontation with police ensued until Abbie Hoffman—a slight figure with unkempt hair he recognised from the newspapers—announced a move to Lincoln Park where the Youth International Party had organised a music festival.

Andrew joined a procession of scruffy hippies, belligerent black-power activists and anti-war demonstrators moving north through Chicago's affluent Miracle Mile towards Lincoln Park. He arrived in time to see a scuffle around a flatbed truck at the park entrance.

Hundreds of people had clambered atop the massive statue of Ulysses S Grant that dominated the park. Andrew gleaned from snippets of conversation that police refused to permit the flatbed into the park for use as a stage for the performers. It was a policy decision that did not go down well with the protesters.

There was more evidence of rising tensions as darkness fell. A tall, lean Black Panther moved through the park, berating the Yippie contingent as 'sell-outs' for submitting to the police curfew. Then a new squad of police arrived and were deployed in skirmish-line formation. Andrew looked on as the same police lieutenant from last night took up his position in front of the police line, announcing through his bullhorn, 'The Lincoln Park precinct will close as of 11 pm. Anyone found within the park after that time will be subject to arrest.'

The police moved forward in unison as Andrew watched with dismay. Some protesters pushed back, throwing any object that came to hand at the oncoming phalanx of Chicago police, leading to a series of running battles, with the police using tear gas and baton charges against the ebb and flow of a hostile crowd. Yet the confrontation at Lincoln Park on the night of Sunday 25 August was a mere skirmish compared with what was to come.

Andrew spent most of the next day in the hotel business

centre, consulting his notes as he started writing his first real news story for *The San Francisco Independent*. He managed to secure a commitment of twenty column inches during a telephone call with Ramsey Thomas that afternoon. Sitting down at one of the business centre's typewriters, he set about crafting the seven hundred words he'd been allocated.

The following day was rather uneventful—frustratingly so for Andrew. The formal opening of the DNC on the far side of town meant that a media presence in Grant and Lincoln parks was sparse to non-existent. On the one hand, this was good for Andrew because there was very little competition from better resourced and more experienced journalists. The big names in media were all over at the International Amphitheatre on 42nd and Halstead covering the nomination of Hubert Humphrey as the Democratic candidate for president. But on the other hand, apart from hippie-flavoured human-interest stories, there was precious little to report.

Andrew wasn't the only one feeling frustrated. Throughout that Tuesday he heard growing rumblings of resentment among protesters about being overshadowed by the 'fuckin' downtown Democrats'. Black Panther, Bobby Seal, gave a fire-and-brimstone speech calling on all protesters to defend themselves with violence, if necessary, against the city's 12,000 police officers on twelve-hour shifts, 7,500 army troops, and 6,000 national guardsmen requested by Daley to aid in keeping order.

As he wandered through the park, Andrew would pick up snippets of conversation among Yippies, Panthers and the newly arrived contingent from the Poor People's Campaign. He approached a group of protesters engaged in heated debate. The more animated speakers were arguing for active resistance to police, while others were insisting that non-violence was still the answer. One boy, who looked as if he still belonged in high school, suddenly erupted in frustration, yelling: 'Fuck the pigs! This is quisling bullshit!'

Passions were rising towards boiling point.

The following day, Wednesday, the focus of the protest shifted back to Grant Park, across the street from Andrew's temporary abode at the Hilton. He tried to gain an interview with Ralph Abernathy, who had stepped in to lead the Southern Christian Leadership Conference, or SCLC, and the Poor People's Campaign after Martin Luther King, Jr's assassination four months earlier.

Abernathy's press adviser had no time for a wet-behind-the-ears journalist from some no-name alternative newspaper in California. But during the course of his failed negotiations with the SCLC press flunky, Andrew did learn that Abernathy had managed to secure a permit to conduct a march that evening to the Amphitheatre where the Democratic Convention was underway.

That afternoon, Andrew followed the flow of people to the Grant Park Band Shell for a protest rally featuring Allen Ginsburg and other prominent protest leaders. Andrew marvelled at the size of the crowd, estimating it to be at least ten thousand strong.

Ginsburg began proceedings by reading a line from his signature poem, *Howl*.

'I saw the best minds of my generation destroyed by madness ...'

Andrew mouthed along, repeating the lines of his favourite poem in time with the author whom he so admired.

Andrew was a bit perplexed when the name David Dellinger was announced over the loudspeakers. Clad in a grey suit and tie, Dellinger looked more like a Madison Avenue ad exec than an anti-war radical, but when Dellinger began to speak, Andrew was impressed to learn that he was a pacifist of long standing who had been imprisoned during the Second World War as a conscientious objector.

Dellinger was in the midst of his remarks when a rumble of outrage came from the crowd.

'What's going on?' Andrew asked his neighbour, a Black Panther with a beret pinned to his hair.

The Panther shrugged.

Andrew watched as Abbie Hoffman walked across the stage and spoke into Dellinger's ear.

Dellinger shook his head in obvious disgust and turned back to the microphone. 'We've just gotten the latest from the DNC. It seems the peace plank amendment to the Democratic platform has been voted down.'

The crowed bellowed in anger.

Dellinger held up his hands, palms outward. 'So, I think ...' he said, pausing until the rumble of discontent subsided, 'I think we should go over to the Amphitheatre and let the Democratic machine know what we think of them. What do you say?'

A massive cheer erupted from the crowd. Andrew watched a young man sprint to a flagpole next to the band shell stage and begin to haul down the Stars and Stripes. He was immediately set upon and arrested by police, who clubbed him into submission before dragging him off in handcuffs. When MOBE leader, Rennie Davis, attempted to intervene, police beat him to the point of unconsciousness as well.

Andrew could sense the pent-up rage in the crowd as protesters streamed out of Grant Park and set off on the long trek to the Amphitheatre. They were almost immediately confronted by a mass of riot police blocking the street. The crowd reacted with uniform defiance. Some protesters began to pelt a patrol car with anything that came to hand.

Tear-gas canisters were picked up and thrown back over the ranks of advancing police, who then charged into the crowd with batons raised. Andrew watched with growing horror as bloodied protesters were wrestled to the ground, handcuffed and frogmarched away by the police.

Almost blinded by floodlights, Andrew squinted so he could see clearly. The lamp was fixed to the camera of a TV news crew that was on the hunt for action. The cameraman found what he sought in the form of a young man with the wisps of a Che Guevara beard who was waving a Viet Cong flag and screaming, 'Revolution, now!'

The chant 'Revolution, now!' spread until it reverberated throughout the crowd confronting lines of riot police along Michigan Avenue near the softball diamonds.

Andrew watched with growing dismay as police tried to confiscate the Viet Cong flag from the hands of the young protester. A melee developed, with the communist banner fluttering over the scene like a Civil War battle flag.

He was changing to his last roll of film when the young flag-bearer began shouting: 'Onto the streets! Onto the streets! The streets belong to the people!' The boy then led a massed charge of protesters into police lines along East Balbo Drive.

Noticing a recessed doorway in a nearby office building, Andrew moved into its shadow, hoping to avoid the attention of police who were responding to protesters' cries of 'Kill the pigs!'. All of the sudden, the police mounted a countercharge of their own, scattering the demonstrators. Andrew watched, appalled, as the police continued their push to corral protesters within the bounds of Grant Park.

Leaving his doorway haven, Andrew outflanked the police through a narrow alley and rejoined the protesters in Grant Park. He saw the tall boy with the Viet Cong flag raise his banner in a gesture of open defiance. The chant of 'Revolution!' resonated through the park. One protester ran back and forth between protesters and police, screaming, 'Welcome to Che Guevara National Park!'

The Viet Cong flag-bearer was catching his breath, leaning against an ancient oak tree. His jet-black hair was cut in a Mohawk-style like something out of a James Fenimore Cooper novel.

'That was very impressive.'

The kid just shrugged.

'How old are you?' Andrew asked, cursing under his breath that he'd just finished his last roll of film.

'Fourteen,' the boy replied, his mouth curving in a smile that was half-bashful, half-proud.

'Wow,' replied Andrew, scribbling in his notebook. 'I'm a journalist from California. Is it okay if I use this in my story?'

The kid smiled. 'Sure. Does that mean I'm gonna be famous?'

Andrew laughed. 'Maybe. So, are you here from out of town for the protest?'

'Nah. I'm from the northside. Belmont and Cicero. It's an Italian neighbourhood.'

'And what's your name? For the story.'

'Micol Lepano,' the kid replied. 'L-e-p-a-n-o.'

'Lepano,' said Andrew. 'Got it. Do your parents know you're out here?'

Micol laughed. 'They've kinda given up trying to control me.'

'I think they'll find out now,' replied Andrew. 'Your flag-waving stunt is going to put your face all over the news.'

'It'll help with the chicks,' smirked Micol, and Andrew couldn't suppress a laugh. But his laughter evaporated at the sight of a three-deep phalanx of Chicago police bulldozing its way through the park.

'You are all in violation of the law,' bellowed a police officer through a bullhorn. 'Vacate the park premises, or face immediate arrest.'

Andrew watched as nobody moved. An uneasy silence settled over the park as TV camera lights were again turned on in anticipation of the looming confrontation.

And then Andrew heard an incongruous sound approaching along Michigan Avenue—the braying of mules and the clop of hooves. The mule train of the Poor People's Campaign was on its authorised march to the DNC at the Amphitheatre.

A few members of the crowd surged forward, mingling with the mules and wagons in the hope of getting through police lines. Andrew followed suit, as the mass of protesters mingled with the Poor People's Campaign members. But the entire mixed cavalcade suddenly came to a halt.

'What's going on?' Andrew asked a bespectacled woman in a sash marked 'Marshal'.

'The freakin' cops are onto us,' the woman said. 'They're saying that only Abernathy's Poor People's Campaign has a march permit. They want everyone else to disperse.'

'What are you going to do?' asked Andrew.

'Who's asking?' she fired back.

Andrew flashed back what he hoped was a disarming smile. 'Journalist.'

The woman nodded and grimaced. 'Well fuck them and fuck that. We've had enough of Daley's shit.'

The chant of 'Pigs, pigs, oink, oink,' erupted from the crowd, followed by a barrage of stones directed at police lines.

Andrew watched a small group of white-shirted officers—lieutenants and captains—who were conferring behind the main line of police. Then a wedge of police suddenly sallied forth and slammed into the crowd. Within seconds, the entire phalanx of police was assailing protesters with their riot batons.

The protesters fought back. Screams of 'Mother-fucking pigs,' and 'Fascist bastards,' filled the night. Andrew moved to one side, trying to retreat from the massive street brawl. He watched in consternation as police responded to verbal taunts with fists, clubs and tear gas.

A young boy was pinned to the trunk of a police cruiser by three police, as another police officer smashed his baton into the lens of a TV camera.

'Hey, man! That's my lens!' protested the shocked cameraman. The police clustered around their lens-breaking comrade and hustled him away behind the phalanx of police. Other officers made a beeline for anyone else in the vicinity holding a camera or notepad.

Then Andrew saw a trio of glowering police moving in his direction with malign intent. He turned away, trying to melt into the human mass of protesters, but hands seized his arms and shoulders, dragging him to the ground.

Andrew had been a bookish sort of kid who avoided contact sports and gave school bullies a wide berth. Having never experienced any sort of physical altercation before, he lay there frozen in panic as his three assailants kicked and beat him. He didn't know how long the beating lasted because a kick to his head knocked him unconscious.

By the time he awoke, Andrew was lying on the floor of a police paddy wagon. The coppery taste of blood filled his mouth and his body's aches formed one agonising whole.

The police van eventually slowed and came to a halt. Moments later the rear doors swung open.

'Time for a walk, hippies,' called a helmeted figure silhouetted against a streetlamp directly behind him.

Andrew was manhandled out of the paddy wagon, which then drove off, leaving him standing with six other bruised protesters in what looked like some sort of industrial area.

'Wh ... where are we?' Andrew asked.

'Indiana Harbor,' spat a short, stocky black man. 'Fuckers took us across the state line and dumped us in fuckin' Indiana Harbor.'

'Where's that?' pressed Andrew. 'How far from the city?'

'Twenty miles or more, that's how far,' said another guy who looked Hispanic.

Andrew groaned. 'What do we do now?'

'What do we do, white boy?' sneered the black man. 'We walk, that's what.'

Dazed with pain, Andrew limped along behind his bedraggled compatriots for what seemed forever. They finally reached what looked like a low-income residential neighbourhood and Andrew flagged down a passing taxi with all the desperation of a man overboard clasping a lifebuoy.

Andrew turned and called, 'Anyone like a lift?', but they shook their heads and plodded on, so Andrew settled into the back of the taxicab with a groan as the driver turned around with a sceptical expression on his face. 'You got cash?' he challenged in an indeterminate Eastern European accent.

Andrew pulled his wallet from his pocket and gave the driver a glimpse of the $20 bills within. The driver nodded and put the cab into gear.

'Where to?'

'Hilton on Michigan Avenue.'

Andrew saw the taxi driver grin in the rear-view mirror.

'You one of those demonstrators making trouble?'

'Journalist,' sighed Andrew. 'Not that it made any difference to the police.'

The taxi driver laughed. 'CPD can be rough bastards, no doubt about it, but this is a rough town.'

'So I've learned,' grimaced Andrew.

'The hard way it seems,' guffawed the driver. 'I have to say, you look like absolute shit.'

Andrew laughed. 'I suppose I do.'

He reached the hotel and sent the driver on his way. Ignoring the stares of hotel guests and staff, he made his way through the lobby to the elevator bank.

On reaching his room, Andrew stripped down and took a long bath. Then he crawled into bed and slept until early afternoon. Picking up the phone, he dialled Ramsey Thomas's direct line.

'Thomas.'

'Hi, Mr Thomas, it's Andrew Lamb.'

'And where the hell have you been? That was a good story you filed a couple of days ago, but I need copy. And I need photos too.'

'Yeah, about that …'

'What the fuck do you mean, about that?' interrupted Thomas. 'Don't tell me you stuffed this up! If you stuffed this up, don't even bother showing your face around here again!'

'Mr Thomas, I was beaten by the police and dumped twenty miles out of town. The bastards took my notebook and camera.'

'Oh! Are you okay?' Thomas asked in a mollified tone.

'A bit bruised, but nothing broken.

'Good to hear. It looked pretty bad on TV. Like a real riot.'

'It was a police riot, Mr Thomas. The police were on a rampage. They were completely out of control.'

'Well, the important thing is you got through it in one piece. Here's what I want you to do. I need seven hundred words by 5 pm my time. I'm giving you front page above the fold for a down-and-dirty piece on what you saw and experienced. Don't worry about photos, we'll get them off the wires. I want a no-holds-barred, firsthand account. And I like the phrase "police riot", so use that in your copy. Can you deliver that?'

'Of course, sir.'

'Good. Then tomorrow morning pack your bags and get to the American counter at O'Hare. There'll be a first-class ticket waiting for you.'

'Th ... thank you, Mr Thomas.'

'Don't thank me, you've earned it. When you're back home we'll have you do a fifteen-hundred-word feature piece that rips the Chicago police a new asshole. Nobody messes with my reporters and gets away with it. So, you'd better get cracking if you're going to meet your deadline.'

'Yes, sir.'

'Oh, and one more thing, Lamb. That sports page job is yours if you still want it.'

Andrew paused for a moment before answering. 'If it's all the same to you, Mr Ramsey, I'd rather stick with politics, if there's a slot for me to fill in the national news section.'

'That's quite a change of view. Are you sure?'

'Yes, sir, I am. There's just too much shit in the world that needs to be uncovered.'

'Kid, if you can get me those seven hundred words by 5 pm you can have any beat you want on *The San Francisco Independent*. And, besides, I think you're going to be a bit of a celebrity. So, just don't run off to the *Chronicle*.'

Andrew laughed. 'Don't worry, sir. I'm happy where I am.'

'Then you'd better get to it. I'll see you on Friday.'

The telephone clicked in Andrew's ear as Ramsey Thomas hung up.

And so, Andrew Lamb dragged himself out of bed, brushed his teeth, dressed and headed down to the Hilton business centre to start work on crucifying Mayor Richard Daley and his police on the front page of *The San Francisco Independent*.

*Chicago Democratic Convention, 1968 — National Guard and Demonstrators
Photo by Fred Mason with Liberation News Service*

10. THE CHICAGO EIGHT CONSPIRACY TRIAL

1969–70

'What's up, boss?' Andrew Lamb asked as he strode into the office of Ramsey Thomas, editor of *The San Francisco Independent*.

'Chicago,' replied Thomas. 'The trial of your Yippie friends is about to start and I want you to cover it.'

'But boss, I'm in the middle of writing that feature piece on the joint resolution to abolish the Electoral College. I spoke to Congressman Talcott and he told me they have the numbers to get it through the House.'

'What about the Senate?' asked Thomas.

'I have a call in to Senator Tunney's office,' Andrew replied.

'Well, put it on the back burner. Even if it passes the House, it'll be weeks before the resolution comes to a vote in the Senate, if it ever does. The fuse on that one is long. It'll still be burning when you get back from Chicago.'

'When do I leave?' Andrew asked.

'The trial opens next Wednesday.'

Andrew glanced at the calendar hanging behind his editor's desk. 'September 24th.'

'Yep,' confirmed Thomas. 'So why don't you fly out there Monday afternoon. That'll give you all of Tuesday to settle in before the circus begins.'

Andrew nodded. 'If the antics of Hoffman and Rubin at the convention are any indication, it'll be a three-ring Barnum & Bailey special.'

'Should make for some great copy,' grinned Thomas. 'Your coverage of the Democratic Convention riots made you a few fans, so build on that.'

'And brought in a few new subscribers to the paper,' replied Andrew, matching Thomas's grin with a smile of his own.

'Don't let that head of yours get too big, boy. Remember, pride ...'

'Goes before a fall,' recited Andrew in unison with his editor. 'So you keep telling me,' he said. 'By the looks of it this trial might take weeks, if not months. I hope you don't expect me to relocate for the duration. My thin Californian blood isn't up to a Chicago winter.'

'We'll play it by ear,' replied Thomas. 'But I definitely want you out there for the opening week. We've booked you a three-star hotel a couple of blocks from the Federal Building. No Hilton this time. The paper won't be able to afford it if you're going to be travelling back and forth. Oh ... and one more thing.'

'Yes?'

'While you're out there, I want you to try and make friends with some of the local Chicago reporters. The ones who'll be covering the trial each and every day.'

'Okay,' replied Andrew. 'But why?'

Thomas sighed the sigh of a frustrated teacher. 'So that if something big happens while you're back here, you'll have someone to call for a firsthand account, of course.'

'Ah,' Andrew replied with a grin. 'Don't worry, I'll be at my charming best.'

Thomas shook his head in mock disgust. 'Get the hell outta my office.'

Andrew was midway out the door when he heard, 'Be careful, okay? Don't get arrested this time.' Thomas was looking at him with a paternal smile.

The following Wednesday morning, Andrew used his press pass to enter the oak-panelled courtroom on the twenty-third floor of the Chicago Federal Building. He had just taken his seat when a door opened behind the judges' bench and a robed figure entered.

'All rise,' the bailiff ordered.

Everyone dutifully rose to their feet, except for the seven white men seated at the defendants table. The eighth defendant—Black Panther Bobby Seale—was the only one of those on trial to comply with the bailiff's direction.

The judge glared at the seated defendants for several seconds before taking his seat and nodding to the bailiff.

'The United States District Court for the Northern District of Illinois is now in session. Judge Julius Jennings Hoffman presiding.'

'The clerk will read the charges,' Judge Hoffmann instructed.

The court clerk, a middle-aged woman with her hair cut in a short bob, put on her glasses and began to read:

> Violation United States Code Title 18, Sections 371, 231 (a) (1) and (0). That the defendants David T Dellinger, Rennard C Davis, Thomas E Hayden, Abbott H Hoffman, Lee Weiner, John R Froines, Jerry C Rubin and Bobby Seale, the defendants herein, did unlawfully, wilfully and knowingly combine, conspire, confederate and agree to commit offences against the

United States, that is: to travel in interstate commerce with the intent to incite, organise, promote, encourage, participate in and carry on a riot and to commit violence in the furtherance of a riot ...

And on it went. A complete recitation of all seven counts that made up the indictment took up the first twenty minutes of the trial. While the clerk droned on, Hoffman, Rubin and their fellow defendants chatted, joked and made an ostentatious show of their contempt for the judicial proceedings.

'Defence counsel will instruct their clients to conduct themselves appropriately,' ordered Judge Hoffman in an irate voice. *For the presiding judge to be so angry so early in the trial was not a good sign,* Andrew thought. *A circus indeed.*

'We'll do our best, Your Honour,' replied William Kunstler, a lawyer already famous—or notorious—for his defence of political radicals.

The odd one out was Bobby Seale, who sat quietly, at least affecting a measure of respect for the judicial proceeding in which he was enmeshed.

Of the eight defendants in the courtroom, Andrew found Seale to be the most interesting. He recalled seeing Seale addressing the crowd in Grant Park just a few hours before that climactic night of police violence on 28 August 1968. But while reading up on the pending trial before boarding his flight to Chicago, Andrew learned that Seale appeared at the DNC protests as a last-minute substitute for Black Panther Eldridge Cleaver and had been in Chicago for less than twenty-four hours. How he could have been part of a conspiracy was puzzling.

It turned out Cleaver was unable to leave California due to

murder charges arising from his alleged role in a shootout with police in Oakland.

After the reading of indictment concluded, the trial moved into the *voir dire* phase, the legal term for jury selection. Andrew watched with growing foreboding as the white defendants continued their theatrical displays of disrespect.

Hoffman and Rubin proved to be picture-perfect stereotypes of the hippy counterculture. They were bearded and clad in headbands, beads, blue jeans and tie-dyed shirts. The defence table was littered with clothing and food wrappers. The white defendants did their best to disrupt proceedings by eating noisily, telling off-colour jokes and offering impertinent unsolicited advice to lawyers, prospective jurors and the judge alike.

At one point, Judge Julius Hoffman took pains to point out that he and defendant Abbie Hoffman were not related, despite their names, at which point Abbie jumped up from the defendants table and shouted, 'Julie, you're making me feel like a poor little orphan!' triggering an outburst of laughter that swept through the courtroom.

By contrast, the prosecution table was a model of good order. US Attorney Thomas Foran and Assistant US Attorney Richard Schultz sat quietly, their ties straight and their suit jackets buttoned. Notebooks and a file of index cards were neatly arranged in front of them.

Andrew looked on as defence attorneys William Kunstler and Leonard Weinglass proposed a long list of questions for potential jurors in the hope of weeding out those with pre-existing biases. They ranged from 'Do you know who Janis Joplin and Jimi Hendrix are?' through to 'Would you let your son or daughter marry a Yippie?' and the provocative 'If your children are female, do they wear brassieres all the time?'

A visibly annoyed Judge Hoffman rejected all but one of the defence questions, allowing the jurors to be asked only whether they had friends or relatives who worked in law enforcement.

Andrew watched, fascinated, as prospective jurors were led into the witness box one by one to be questioned and challenged by the lawyers of either side. Some of the jury candidates stared in disbelief at the antics of Hoffman and Rubin, which were entirely at odds with their preconceived notions of courtroom practice, no doubt taken from television re-runs of *Perry Mason* and the like.

Each legal team was allowed a number of 'peremptory challenges' during jury selection, meaning it could disqualify potential jurors at will.

The prosecution almost immediately invoked a peremptory challenge to bump a black man from the jury. He was an electrician by trade, which demonstrated he was smart. Andrew could see no other reason for his exclusion from the jury except the fact that he was black and he was male.

The prosecution also removed a recent graduate from the University of Illinois. Andrew concluded that prosecutors saw a 'college boy' as someone who might be sympathetic towards the defendants. But they then allowed two middle-aged black women to be seated on the jury. *Apparently,* Andrew thought sourly, *it wouldn't do for the prosecution to exhibit too much overt racial prejudice.*

After a half day of questioning and legal challenges, a jury of two white men and ten women—two black and eight white—was empanelled. Throughout the *voir dire* process, Andrew kept an eye on Bobby Seale. He watched as Seale grimaced in disgust at the most transparent manoeuvrings of the prosecution to secure a supportive jury.

The second day of the trial kicked off with yet more high drama as Bobby Seale rose from his seat before opening arguments began and strode to the lectern.

Andrew watched intently as Judge Hoffman said by way of challenge, 'Just a minute, sir. Who is your attorney?'

Seale looked straight at Judge Hoffman and declared: 'If I'm denied my right to legal defence counsel of my choice, then I can only see this entire trial as blatantly racist.'

Andrew later learned that Seale was referring to Judge Hoffman's rejection of a request for a continuance—legal speak for a postponement—of six weeks. Seale's preferred lawyer, Charles Garry, was in urgent need of gall-bladder surgery and would be out of commission for more than a month. When Seale appealed, Judge Hoffman's ruling was upheld by a panel of judges from the Seventh Circuit Court of Appeals.

A visibly indignant Judge Hoffman declared, 'Watch what you say, sir!'

But Seale was heedless, proclaiming his intention to appear *pro se*—legal speak for representing himself at trial.

Prosecutor Thomas Foran shot to his feet, proclaiming his objection.

Judge Hoffman denied Seale's request, triggering a gasp of disbelief from the defence team.

Seale leaned across the defence table. 'What about my constitutional rights? Can't a man defend himself?'

'In Mr Kunstler you have a very able lawyer to speak for you,' Judge Hoffman replied.

'I remind Your Honour that I've been dismissed by Mr Seale,' replied Kunstler. 'I am unable to make any statement on my former client's behalf.'

'Don't play games with me, Counsellor,' chided Judge Hoffman. 'You filed a notice of appearance for the defendant Robert Seale. I will not permit Seale to hijack this proceeding by making an opening statement with his very competent lawyer seated there.'

At this point, a man whom Andrew hadn't yet seen made his way from the gallery to the defence table. 'Your Honour, Thomas Sullivan on behalf of defence attorneys Gerald Lefcourt, Michael Kennedy, Dennis Roberts and Michael Tigar. I ask the court to accept their motion of withdrawal from the case.' It seemed that, for some unexplained reason, Judge Hoffman thought that the four attorneys who had withdrawn from the case should represent Bobby Seale.

Judge Hoffman frowned. 'For what reason?'

'Your Honour, they have a conflicting timetable. All defendants except Mr Seale are agreeable to the withdrawal of Mr Lefcourt, Mr Kennedy, Mr Roberts and Mr Tigar.'

'And where are those gentlemen now?' challenged Judge Hoffman. 'Why aren't they here to file this motion on their own behalf?'

'Your Honour, all I can say is that Mr Lefcourt has discussed this matter with the defendant, Mr Hoffman, who is happy to be represented by Mr Weinglass.'

'I don't care to participate in negotiations,' barked Judge Hoffman. 'Before I consider this motion there will be a finding that the respondents, Michael E Tigar and Gerald B Lefcourt, Michael J Kennedy and Dennis J Roberts, are in contempt of this court. I am not going to have lawyers flout the authority of this court.'

'May I be heard?' interceded Sullivan.

'I commit them without bail,' growled Judge Hoffman. 'I deny the motion for bail.'

'Your Honour, are they to remain in custody?'

'Yes,' barked Hoffman.

'For the rest of their lives?' challenged Sullivan.

'I will determine on the disposition of this case on Monday morning at ten o'clock,' the judge announced.

Andrew was staggered by this bizarre response from the judge. He assumed there must be some reason for it, but what that could be was a mystery.

The high drama surrounding Bobby Seale and the defence lawyers being held in contempt was lightened by the clownish antics of the seven white defendants. Abbie Hoffman gave a one-fingered salute while pleading not guilty and Thomas Hayden saluted the jury with a clenched fist. When Judge Hoffman admonished Hayden for 'shaking his fist' at the jury, Hayden replied 'It's my customary greeting, Your Honour.'

When Assistant US Attorney Richard Schultz complained about Abbie Hoffman's habit of standing and blowing a kiss to the jury, the judge declared, 'The jury is directed to disregard the kiss from Mr Hoffman,' triggering another gale of laughter throughout the courtroom.

As Assistant US Attorney Schultz began to speak about Bobby Seale, Andrew chuckled as the Black Panther leader waved to the jury like the Pope from the balcony of St Peter's Square. It was hard to take proceedings seriously given the antics of the accused. But Schultz claimed Seale had incited people to arm themselves and riot. An undercover police officer claimed Seale had made a speech in Lincoln Park and encouraged protesters to 'barbecue some pork'. Andrew made a note of it, but he felt uneasy about the trial, and it had hardly begun.

When the time came for opening arguments by the defence,

Leonard Weinglass told the jurors in a stern voice that they were 'the highest authority'. Andrew was surprised to hear this, assuming the judge was the highest authority, but Weinglass enlarged on his initial statement by outlining the English and American traditions that backed his view, particularly in cases involving religious or political beliefs.

A visibly fuming Judge Hoffman suddenly interrupted Weinglass and excused the jury for a fifteen-minute break. He then turned and admonished Weinglass for his 'contumacious conduct'.

Andrew jotted down the word 'contumacious' in his notes as a reminder to consult the dictionary for a precise definition later, but he had already inferred that the word's meaning wasn't good for the defence case. Perhaps Weinglass was outraged by the treatment meted out to the other defence attorneys.

Weinglass continued his presentation under the gimlet eye of the judge.

After Judge Hoffman called a recess for lunch, Andrew sat in the courtroom, watching a pretty, red-haired young woman scribbling furiously in her notebook.

'Are you a reporter?' he asked, edging towards her.

She glanced up from her notebook in momentary annoyance before continuing to take notes. 'Lena Koslowski, *Sun-Times*,' she said, her head bowed as she wrote.

'Andrew Lamb, *The San Francisco Independent*,' he replied. He waited while she finished her notetaking.

'So, welcome to Chicago,' she said eventually.

Andrew laughed. 'Thanks. Wonderful city you've got, but it's not my first visit. Last time I was here the cops beat the crap outta me and dumped me at Indiana Harbor.'

'At the DNC?'

Andrew nodded.

Lena laughed. 'So, you've been the beneficiary of our famous CPD hospitality.'

'I have. You're a local, then?'

'Pulaski Park born and bred,' she nodded. 'Except for four years up in Evanston at Northwestern.'

'UC Berkeley, myself. So, ah … I don't mean to be forward, but, given that you're a hometown girl and I'm an outta-town guy, perhaps you might show me around a bit? During my last trip all I got to see was Grant Park and …'

'Indiana Harbor,' she interjected with a smile.

She stood there in silence, appraising Andrew with a cool, calculating gaze. 'Dinner. My choice, your bill,' she said finally.

'You mean the *Independent's* bill,' grinned Andrew.

'No slumming, then. I hope you like steak.'

'Love it.'

'Good, 'cause we're going to Gene & Gorgetti's, the best steakhouse in Chicago.'

'It's a date,' said Andrew.

'Oh, is it now?' replied Lena, her brows arching.

'Yes, it is,' affirmed Andrew. 'And to seal the deal I'll treat you to the best taqueria in the Bay Area when you come to visit. You haven't eaten real Mexican food if you haven't been to El Hidalgo.'

'So, I'm coming to California, am I?' asked Lena, her smile now decidedly coquettish. 'Well, don't get ahead of yourself, mister. We'll see how tonight goes.'

Their flirtatious banter was interrupted by the bailiff's call that the trial was resuming.

Raymond Simon, Corporation Counsel for the City of Chicago and the prosecution's initial witness, spoke about permits required during the Democratic Convention to assemble in streets and parks. But the proceedings that afternoon were repeatedly interrupted by objections from Kunstler and Weinglass.

Andrew and Lena—they were now sitting together in the gallery—exchanged looks of dismay as Judge Hoffman overruled every single objection.

A middle-aged, moustachioed man seated beside Lena on the other side leaned over and whispered in her ear.

After a few moments she leaned towards Andrew in response to his quizzical glance.

'That's Professor Jon Walz of Northwestern Law,' she whispered. 'He knows Judge Hoffman personally and says the whole trial is way out of bounds. He says Hoffman's bias is laying the groundwork for the entire case to be nullified on appeal.'

Andrew nodded and continued watching the campaign by Assistant US Attorney Schultz to portray the eight defendants as the greatest threat to American national security since Lenin.

By the morning of Monday 28 September, public consternation about Judge Hoffman's jailing of the four defence lawyers reached a fever pitch. Newspapers across the country featured front-page accounts of how federal marshals had arrested Michael Tigar in California, and flown him to Chicago where he spent the night in jail. And how, later, Tigar was joined in his cell by Gerald Lefcourt.

A federal court in San Francisco had already set aside Judge Hoffman's contempt orders for two of the lawyers, Roberts and Kennedy, because an offence had not been specified. That Monday morning, a hastily convened panel of the Seventh Circuit Court of Appeals moved to quash Judge Hoffman's contempt rulings against Tigar and Lefcourt.

This whole episode shocked Andrew Lamb to his core and compounded the trauma he had suffered at the hands of the Chicago police the previous year.

The only salve to his soul was Lena Koslowski, with whom he found himself spending every minute of his spare time throughout that week in Chicago. That one dinner turned into daily breakfasts and lunches, and overnight lovemaking soon followed.

The French called it *coup de foudre*. In his NYT bestseller *The Godfather*—which Andrew had just finished—Mario Puzo described it as 'the thunderbolt'. Whatever the name, his feelings towards Lena were growing deeper by the day. By the time he had to return to California, Andrew Lamb had acquired both a steady girlfriend and a serious source of first-hand information on the trial.

From Berkeley, Andrew would call each evening to whisper sweet nothings and hear about the day's happenings in Judge Hoffman's courtroom. Then he would labour into the night over his notes to churn out anything from four hundred to seven hundred words of copy for the next day's edition.

Often what he heard and then wrote was comic. Andrew and Lena laughed together over two thousand miles of telephone wire when she told him how one day Jerry Rubin and Abbie Hoffman walked into the courtroom wearing judges' robes. When the Yippie duo obeyed the irate command to doff the judicial attire, they turned out to be wearing Chicago police uniforms underneath. The entire courtroom exploded in laughter.

But there was a more serious side to the trial as well. Lena was outraged when two jurors received letters at their homes with the threat 'You are being watched, signed, The Black Panthers', scrawled in black felt pen.

She told Andrew how Bobby Seale was disdainful of the notion that the letters constituted a real threat. He, instead, argued that this was the work of *agents provocateurs* who sought to prejudice the jury against him.

At the end of the day Judge Hoffman decided to dismiss one of the two jurors, and an alternate was sworn in her place.

Kunstler vehemently protested, because the dismissed juror was in her twenties, while the new juror was middle-aged. Lena thought this change of jurors might be a plot by the prosecution to purge from the jury anyone prosecutors suspected might be sympathetic to the defence.

With his cynicism towards the prosecution growing by the day, Andrew agreed. He was growing increasingly cynical about America, too, which fuelled a waxing radicalisation of his politics. He was further outraged when Lena told him that the upshot of the letter's affair was a decision to sequester the jury.

As the trial progressed, it became clear that the prosecution's case rested largely on the testimony of several undercover cops and *agents provocateurs*. Chicago police officer Robert Pierson managed to talk his way into the role of Abbie Hoffman's bodyguard. Pierson testified on the stand that on 28 August, Hoffman had proclaimed his intention to: 'Hold the park. We're going to fuck up the pigs and the convention.' Other undercover police testified about plans by the radical Students for a Democratic Society to sow mayhem throughout downtown Chicago.

Lena told Andrew that Kunstler's cross-examination was very effective in pressuring these undercover agents to concede that these statements might have been wild talk rather than concrete plans of action. In fact, by mid-October, Lena was relating that the defence team seemed to have made a decision to change strategy. She reported that, over recent days, Kunstler and Weinglass spoke more about the political issues that motivated the DNC protests. The Vietnam War, the assassinations of Robert Kennedy and Martin Luther King, Jr, took front and centre place in the defence arguments.

Meanwhile, Bobby Seale hadn't wavered in his desire to represent himself or secure his own counsel of choice. As October wore on, Lena told Andrew that Seale's self-restraint was eroding. She described how the Black Panther would repeatedly burst into tirades in open court in which he labelled Judge Hoffman, a 'fascist dog', a 'pig' and a 'racist'.

Finally, on 29 October, it was the turn of Judge Hoffman to lose his temper. Enraged by one of Seale's sudden outbursts, Hoffman ordered Seale bound and gagged in full public view. The tidal wave of media outrage was immediate and overwhelming. Andrew and Lena commiserated telephonically when, on 5 November, Hoffman severed the Seale prosecution from the case against the other defendants, sentencing him to four years' imprisonment for contempt.

'And thus, not with a bang but a whimper, the Chicago Eight become the Chicago Seven,' intoned Andrew.

'T S Elliot,' said Lena over the phone. 'Are you trying to woo me with the power of your intellect?' she teased.

'I'll use anything that comes to hand,' Andrew replied, hoping she could feel the wattage of his smile over two thousand miles.

Over the next few weeks, the trial entered the doldrums with little of interest to report. Andrew moved on to cover other stories, but kept in nightly touch with Lena, using the pretext of the trial to sheet home the phone bill to the *Independent*.

He continued to write the occasional piece about the Chicago

Seven, and was interested to read in November that Eldridge Cleaver had escaped to Cuba, and later Algeria, to avoid criminal prosecution. In early December he penned an article arguing that the prosecution case was weak enough to make the prospect of a hung jury possible.

From mid-December to the third week of January, the defence team brought forward a stellar list of celebrities as character witnesses. Long queues for tickets to the gallery suddenly materialised with fans eager to see their favourite artists at close quarters. Norman Mailer, Pete Seeger, Judy Collins, Arlo Guthrie and LSD guru Timothy Leary all made an appearance. But the trial again turned nasty during its final two weeks.

Ramsey Thomas was so happy with the copy Andrew was producing from afar that he didn't feel the need to pay for another trip to Chicago, much to the mutual chagrin of Andrew and Lena. This meant Andrew wasn't in the courtroom to watch the trial descend into hostile chaos, marked by intemperate outbursts by the seven defendants and blatantly biased rulings by Judge Hoffman. Lena, who was there, counted forty-eight citations of contempt handed down by the judge before the trial ended.

During final summations, the prosecution argued that the Chicago Seven were dangerous anarchists, citing unproved allegations of a Yippie plot to lace the Chicago water supply with LSD.

By contrast, Kunstler portrayed the defendants as idealists who fought back in self-defence against vengeful police. He derided the idea that there had been any conspiracy, quoting the defence testimony of writer Norman Mailer who said, 'Left-wingers are incapable of conspiracy because they're all egomaniacs.' Lena and Andrew laughed when she reminded him of Abbie Hoffman's quip during his testimony— 'Conspiracy? Hell, we couldn't agree on lunch.'

Kunstler's strategy of pushback on the conspiracy charge proved to be the right call when the jury returned a verdict of 'not guilty' on that charge for all seven defendants. But Jerry Rubin, Abbie Hoffman, David Dellinger, Tom Hayden and Rennie Davis were found 'guilty' of crossing a state border with intent to incite a riot. John Froines and Lee Weiner were acquitted of all charges.

On the afternoon of the next day—20 February 1970—Andrew received a call from a breathless Lena who broke the news that Judge Hoffman had imposed a sentence of five years' imprisonment and a $5,000 fine on each of the guilty five. Hoffman had imposed lengthy jail sentences for contempt on every one of the Chicago Seven, plus lawyers Kunstler and Weinglass.

Andrew was appalled and channelled his outrage into a thundering column that ran on the front page of the next day's edition of the *Independent*. The most widely quoted paragraph from that piece read:

> Judge Julius Hoffman is a disgrace to the principles of American justice. And if he adds me to the list of those he charges with contempt, my only response will be, 'Yes, that word accurately describes my attitude towards you and the way you have debased the court over which you preside'.

The article scored Andrew an invitation to address a protest rally that evening at UC Berkeley's Boalt Hall, much to Ramsey Thomas's delight.

'It's a great opportunity for the paper,' enthused Thomas. 'The auditorium will be filled with our kind of people, each of whom is a potential subscriber. I want you to get up there and tell your story ... and plug the *Independent* while you do so.'

Andrew grinned. 'Don't worry, boss, I'll tell them how my wise and noble editor had the vision to send me halfway across the country to cover the DNC.'

'Don't push your luck, kid,' said Thomas with a smile of paternal affection. 'Sucking up will avail you not. You'll get a raise when I'm good and ready to give it to you.'

The following evening Andrew Lamb swallowed down the butterflies in his stomach and took to the podium before a crowd of several hundred people. He began to speak without notes, telling of his experiences during the convention and what he saw at the trial of the Chicago Seven.

Then suddenly, the door opened, and a flash of red hair appeared at the rear of the auditorium. Andrew paused for a few moments, unsure as to what he was seeing, until Lena Koslowski looked up at him with a thousand-watt smile.

He recovered his composure and completed his remarks to a standing ovation and handshakes from his fellow speakers. But he had no interest in public plaudits and he moved away through the crowd towards the red hair.

'I see you're famous now,' she said with a disarming smile as he approached.

Andrew swept her into his arms, and they kissed.

'What are you doing here?' he asked in wonder.

Lena shrugged. 'Trial was over, and I wanted to come and see that glorious Californian weather for myself.'

'That's the only reason? The weather?'

Lena flashed him a smile. 'There may have been a few other factors,' she teased.

Andrew laughed, slipping his arm into hers. 'Let's get the hell outta here. I owe you a Mexican dinner and my car is just around the corner in the parking lot.'

Looking like a committed couple, they strode arm in arm out into the winter Bay Area night.

Life was good—and promised to get even better.

END NOTE

On 11 May 1972, the Seventh Circuit Court of Appeals quashed all of Judge Hoffman's contempt citations, ruling that any finding of contempt that resulted in over six months in prison required a jury trial. Later that year, on 21 November, the same appeals court reversed the Riot Act guilty verdicts against Rubin, Hoffman, Dellinger, Davis and Hayden.

As Professor Jon Walz of Northwestern Law predicted, the appellate court based its ruling on Judge Hoffman's refusal to permit inquiry into the cultural biases of potential jurors during *voir dire*. The appeals court also criticised Judge Hoffman's 'deprecatory and often antagonistic attitude toward the defence'.

But most outrageous, from a civil liberties perspective, was the finding that the FBI, with the knowledge and complicity of Judge Hoffman and prosecutors, had bugged the offices of Kunstler and Weinglass. The Court of Appeals panel said it had 'little doubt but that the wrongdoing of FBI agents would have required reversal of the convictions on the substantive charges'.

Seven Chicago police officers charged with violating the civil rights of demonstrators during the 1968 DNC riots were acquitted during a different trial. Charges against an eighth officer were dismissed. When later asked about these acquittals, Assistant US Attorney Richard Shultz simply observed that, 'The people who sit on juries in this city are just not ready to convict a Chicago policeman.'

11. BRING THE TROOPS HOME

NOVEMBER 1969

> 'Sarge, I'm only eighteen, I got a ruptured spleen,
> And I always carry a purse
> I've got eyes like a bat and my feet are flat
> My asthma's getting worse.'

The lyrics of Phil Ochs's counterculture classic *The Draft Dodger Rag* echoed through the bus as it came to a halt behind a column of similar vehicles parked along the narrow, tree-lined street. It was just after noon on Friday 14 November 1969.

'All right, people, listen up!' Arthur Sillitoe was president of the Williams College Students for a Democratic Society, or SDS. He pointed across a small park towards a six-storey, greystone building. 'That's Copley Hall. Our SDS colleagues from the Georgetown University chapter have been kind enough to let us crash there while we're here in DC. We'll probably be bedding down in the halls, so I hope you all brought your sleeping-bags. This is also the spot where we'll be leaving for the return trip to North Adams on Sunday morning at 10 am sharp. We won't wait, so don't be late. Any questions?'

None were forthcoming.

'Let's get to it then.'

Sillitoe led us off the bus into Copley Hall and we were guided to a room on the second floor where we dumped our gear in a pile.

'We'll reconvene at the front entrance in twenty minutes. If you need a pit stop, take it now.'

The twenty-eight-strong Williams College SDS contingent reassembled at the appointed time and we set off south through the cobblestone streets of Georgetown towards the Potomac. The weather was cold, but nothing like the bitter winters that were a staple part of life in western Massachusetts. Crossing Francis Scott Key Bridge into Virginia, we made our way as a group to Arlington National Cemetery. There, we were each issued with a candle and small sign featuring the name and date of death of an American Vietnam War casualty. Mine read, 'Rudolph Aguilar 11 August 1965'.

With our candles lit, we joined a procession of thousands who marched silently across the Theodore Roosevelt Bridge over the Potomac. There was something spectral about the sight of flickering candles held by myriad hands moving in soundless accord past the Lincoln Memorial to the White House. From there we strode down Pennsylvania Avenue to the foot of Capitol Hill. The 'March Against Death'—as this event had been titled—broadcast a powerful message of popular discontent with the war in Vietnam—all without a single word being uttered.

Among the milling crowd around the Capitol Reflecting Pool, I lost touch with the rest of the Williams contingent, but I wasn't worried. Having spent three years in DC during the early 60s when my dad worked as an adviser to Douglas Dillon, JFK's treasury secretary, I knew the city well.

I never made it back to Georgetown that night, instead spending hours chatting, drinking and smoking pot with new acquaintances among my fellow protesters. I met people from all parts of the country and all walks of life. There were middle-aged professionals—teachers, architects and lawyers—along with unionised auto and steel workers and people from California and Oregon who had driven across the country to add their voices to the call for an end to the war.

As morning broke on 15 November, I was tired but determined to play my part in what promised to be the largest anti-war protest in American history. But it was hardly the first of its kind. Over the previous eighteen months there had been a series of demonstrations that had ranged from the serious to the farcical.

The National Mobilisation to End the War in Vietnam orchestrated a protest event in April 1967 that brought thousands of activists to DC. Then, that same October, counterculture icons Abbie Hoffman and Jerry Rubin led a mass exercise in political agitprop by surrounding the Pentagon with a crowd of demonstrators who tried to levitate the building into the air. Novelist Norman Mailer's personal account of the October 1967 demonstration—including his arrest outside the Pentagon—won him a Pulitzer Prize.

In terms of political influence, the anti-war movement was now considered more than a noisy minority of disloyal leftist radicals. Just the previous year, pro-Vietnam War 'Ballad of the Green Berets' was named the number one single of 1966 by *Billboard* magazine. But most Americans retained their faith in what the government described as the campaign to halt communist expansionism.

The watershed moment in American public attitudes towards the war came during the North Vietnamese Tet Offensive in

January 1968. Video footage of the US embassy in Saigon under siege by Viet Cong suicide squads shattered public confidence in the prospect of American victory. The nation's most influential journalist, CBS newsreader Walter Cronkite, proclaimed on air that the war was a lost cause. A few weeks later, President Lyndon Baines Johnson announced he would not seek re-election. America seemed engulfed by a horrific cycle of assassinations, race riots and political turmoil.

But despite—or perhaps because of—the civil unrest marking 1968 a horrible year, Republican Richard Nixon won the presidency in an Electoral College landslide on a platform of law and order. Notwithstanding this political setback, the anti-war movement was undeterred. At this stage of the war, the United States was losing over five hundred troops 'killed in action' each month. Each evening, news broadcasts ended with a seemingly endless parade of portraits of the newly dead. The first Moratorium to End the War in Vietnam took place on 15 October 1969, with an estimated 250,000 protesters marching in Washington and thousands more following suit throughout the world.

On 3 November, President Nixon responded to the first moratorium with a polemical counterattack in the form of his famous 'silent majority' speech that portrayed the anti-war movement as soft on communism. Initial public reaction to the speech was positive, with the White House switchboard overwhelmed by incoming calls of congratulations. It appeared the anti-war movement was faltering against a wave of patriotic support for the war. Then, on 12 November 1969, investigative journalist Seymour Hersh broke the story of the massacre in a Vietnamese village called Mỹ Lai where rogue US troops slaughtered over two hundred civilians.

Historians usually dispute the fallacy 'post hoc ergo propter hoc', which means, 'since event B followed event A, B must have been caused by A'. So, of course, it can't be proven that the revelations of massacre and subsequent cover-up led to the second moratorium being even larger than the first, but the statistics speak for themselves. The second moratorium brought roughly 500,000 demonstrators to Washington in November, double the number of the previous month. On a personal note, I can say that Mỹ Lai played a big part in my ultimate decision to make the four-hundred-mile trip from North Adams, Massachusetts, to Washington DC. A seat on the Williams College bus cost $40, quite a sizeable sum to someone on a student budget in the late 1960s but, after Mỹ Lai, I felt it was something I had to do.

The smell of coffee and baked goods wafted through the air and I followed my nose towards the source. I saw that the American Friends Service Committee, a Quaker organisation, had set up a tent on the mall where a group of middle-aged women were distributing cups of coffee and what appeared to be sandwiches. Stomach growling, I joined the line and was able get the last dregs of coffee. I just missed the last of the corned beef on rye. No matter. I would think about food later. In the meantime, I would make do with caffeine.

People nearby were talking in outraged tones about a clash between protesters and police that had apparently taken place overnight around at Dupont Circle, due east of the university. Some of the language being used was far too radical for my taste. While I opposed the Vietnam War as an intrusion by the United States into the internal affairs of another country, I didn't think anything positive would be accomplished by describing police as 'pigs'.

At around 10 am that Saturday 15 November, numbers began

to swell at 3rd Street NW. By noon, the size of the crowd could only be described as massive. Estimates by *The Washington Post* and *The New York Times* put the number of protesters at over 500,000. At the time, all I knew was that we could only shuffle rather than walk because there were so many people crammed together.

As I came abreast of the red-brick Smithsonian Castle, the faint sound of music emerged, ebbing and flowing with gusts of the wind. Edging my way across 15th Street towards the Washington Monument, I soon recognised the distinctive voice of Pete Seeger being broadcast through large speakers placed around the obelisk.

Members of the crowd were brandishing banners and placards with messages ranging from humorous to serious or outright seditious. The one I had chosen was simple. It read, 'Stop the War', while others said things like, 'Girls Say Yes to Men Who Say No'. All well and good.

For reasons of both ethics and pragmatism I was uncomfortable with the brandishing of Viet Cong flags and calls for Marxist revolution by the more radical cohort of protesters. I was against the Vietnam War, not because I hated America, but because I loved it. Our involvement in South-East Asia was an unwinnable exercise in futility that was dragging my country towards brutality and costing lives and money that the United States could ill afford.

The political radicalism on display at the moratorium was also self-defeating in a pragmatic sense. America's war in Vietnam would only be ended through the application of grassroots political pressure. Wooing a majority of mainstream voters to our side of the argument was necessary if that end were ever to be achieved. But we would never win mainstream support if the American public saw protesters waving flags of an enemy who was, at that very moment, killing young American soldiers. I had no patience for such self-indulgent posturing.

I must also confess to an element of self-interest in my anti-war activism. I was midway through my senior year at Williams. This made me consider what would happen after my student deferment expired on graduation some six months hence.

I recall reading somewhere that the Selective Service—the formal name for the military draft—took over 280,000 young Americans into the armed services in 1969. As I was sound of mind and body, two years of military service was more likely than not, although being drafted didn't necessarily mean combat duty as an infantryman in Vietnam. There were other options, such as volunteering for the navy, air force or coast guard. As a university graduate in the sciences, it would be easy for me to snag some sort of cushy lower-echelon desk job, but I was uncomfortable with the thought of gaming the system while other less-privileged Americans my age were dispatched into the meat-grinder of war. I would take my medicine if and when it came. Truth be told, a big part of the reason I was in Washington that day was to forestall this potential outcome by helping to end the war.

Around 4 pm I accepted the gracious offer of a hoagie sandwich from a girl who noticed the covetous glances I was casting towards her stash of food. Starvation was averted. As quid pro quo, I offered her the sweater I was wearing beneath my heavy, shearling coat. I was dressed for a New England winter and she was shivering with cold beneath a University of North Carolina sweatshirt and light army surplus jacket. I think we both felt it was a fair trade.

She wasn't the only one who was underdressed. It appeared to me that most of those around me were more concerned about radical chic than practicality. Olive drab army field jackets adorned with peace symbols and political buttons were the unofficial uniform of the day. These people may have been trembling from the cold, but at least they looked the part of revolutionary activists from central casting.

Towards evening, I manoeuvred through the mass of people across the Ellipse to the White House fence, arriving just as the Washington Metropolitan Police announced the protest permit had expired. So, I began to wander back down Pennsylvania Avenue towards Capitol Hill. Almost twenty-four hours had elapsed since I'd seen anyone from Williams. The excitement of being part of the largest anti-war protest in history was enough to keep my fatigue at bay ... for now.

I saw a raucous crowd assembled in front of the Justice Department, with a phalanx of police arrayed to protect the building. I didn't see who triggered the outbreak of violence, whether it was radicals among the protesters or an overreaction by law enforcement, but I arrived just as police fired a barrage of tear-gas canisters. It was my first experience of what is euphemistically described as the 'riot control agents', and it was horrible.

My eyes and sinuses burned and I couldn't catch my breath. I staggered across Pennsylvania Avenue to escape the billowing clouds of tear gas.

'Over here,' I heard. Blinded by tears, I could see nothing until I was comforted by a hand on my arm gently guiding me to, I knew not where.

'Sit down and put your head up,' the voice instructed.

Still blind, I knelt and felt rough concrete under my palms. I sat down and lifted my face skywards. I blinked involuntarily as cold liquid splashed into my eyes. The tear-gas symptoms began to diminish almost immediately.

After about a minute, the blurred image of my saviour came into focus. A middle-aged, bearded man looking down at me with a benevolent expression.

'Milk,' he told me with a grin, raising a carton into my field of view. 'It's the best thing for tear gas.'

'Thanks,' I coughed. 'You sound as though you speak from experience.'

He laughed. 'I'm a communist from way back. I've been tear-gassed from Selma, Alabama, to Syracuse, New York.'

'Well thank you, comrade,' I joked.

'Solidarity forever,' he replied, raising a clenched fist. 'But I should go. You're not the only one coughing his guts out.'

I nodded, sitting quietly as I watched him attend to other tear-gas victims.

That was it for me. I was hurting, tired, and in need of a toilet—I couldn't quite bring myself to empty my bladder on the streets of Washington. At that moment I didn't give a hoot about the Nixon administration.

I walked north to K Street and then west to Georgetown. At Rock Creek Park I ducked behind some bushes and took care of my full bladder. My next stop was a pizza shop on Wisconsin Avenue where, after washing my hands, I bought three slices of pepperoni.

It was early when I arrived back at Copley Hall, but the building was still abuzz with activity. Students wearing the slogans of a dozen colleges and universities milled around, talking, eating and smoking. Despite the lateness of the hour, the atmosphere was electric, but my lack of sleep was finally catching up with me. I made my way to the Williams room on the second floor, found my backpack, unfurled my sleeping-bag and crawled inside. Within minutes I was dead to the world.

I slept until a hand on my shoulder woke me.

'We thought we'd lost you,' said Arthur Sillitoe. 'What were you up to?'

I blinked my eyes into focus. 'Wandered around the mall. Went to the White House. Got myself tear-gassed at the Justice Department.'

'Wow,' said Sillitoe, his head nodding in a gesture of newfound respect, 'that sounds wild. I can see that your eyes are still bloodshot as hell. But now it's up and at 'em. We're leaving in forty-five minutes, so you just have time to shower and grab some breakfast. I expect a full account when we're on the bus.'

'Thanks, Arthur,' I mumbled. Groping around in my backpack I found a towel, fresh clothes and a toothbrush and headed off for a shower. After an omelette sandwich, I decided to stretch my legs and get some fresh air, so I crossed Copley Lawn to 37th Street NW in search of the Williams College bus. Most of my fellows were already there and they began to bombard me with questions even before I had a chance to sit down.

During the conversation that followed, I discovered that the other 'Ephs'—the nickname for a Williams student—mostly stuck together and had an uneventful time. After the moratorium, they returned to Georgetown and slept in until around midday. Early on Saturday afternoon, they hoofed it to the Washington Monument, and spent the day listening to Pete Seeger, Peter Paul and Mary, and Arlo Guthrie, son of the legendary folk singer Woody Guthrie.

Arthur Sillitoe led the questioning, demanding that I recount every detail as if he wanted to experience vicariously what I had gone through.

When I protested that it wasn't that big a deal; that it was simply the happenstance of being in the right (or wrong) place at the right (or wrong) time to be tear-gassed, I was accused of false modesty.

After our return to campus, the story of my tear-gassing outside the Justice Department was burnished in the telling and retelling. I suddenly found myself transformed from an anonymous chemistry major to something of a campus celebrity. I must confess that after a while I began to enjoy my newfound status, particularly in terms of my batting average with the opposite sex, but my laurels faded. The world turned and I reverted to my former status of a mild-mannered chemistry major.

I dealt with my personal challenge of military service by simply extending my student deferment through further study. Never having been out of the US, I had a bad case of travel itch, and my *magna cum laude* BSc gained me admission to a number of graduate programs in Europe. For reasons of linguistic convenience and ethnic heritage, I ultimately chose the University of Edinburgh, where I spent the next five years pursuing a doctorate in chemical engineering. By the time I returned to the US as a newly minted PhD, the Vietnam War was over.

Prior to the second Moratorium to End the Vietnam War in November 1969, I had never been particularly political. I've been honest enough to concede the element of self-interest that was part of my decision to take part in the Washington protest. Yet I never doubted the essential justice of the anti-war cause, even though, as a nation, we appear to have learned little. In the years since, I have watched as America has endured what seemed to be endless cycles of domestic corruption, Watergate, women's and gay rights, economic crises and foreign adventurism.

I have been fortunate that my profession enabled me to tune out much of what blights our world. Within the sterile confines of the lab, I could concentrate on the unyielding principles of the scientific method. After thirty years of work mostly on new pharmaceutical drugs, I retired to a hilltop house outside Santa Fe, New Mexico. Along the way I met and married an architect, who subsequently designed our home—and had four children who, in turn, produced nine grandchildren.

I write this as a septuagenarian who is in the autumn, or even winter, of his life. From that perspective, I confess that thoughts of legacy and life impact have begun to intrude on my mind with greater frequency.

Family, of course, is my most important contribution to this world. My children are all very different, but each of them is a fine person who makes me proud. My thirty-year career in pharmaceuticals is also the source of much satisfaction. While only a small cog in a much larger machine, I can still take pride in my contribution to the development of drugs that improved and saved many lives.

Of late, I have also begun to ponder the November 1969 moratorium. Those ponderings are the genesis of this personal account. I believed at the time that half a million protesters engulfing Washington would generate irresistible pressure for an immediate end to the war. How naïve I was.

I remain proud of the stand I took that day. Those protests helped bring the war to an end. So, we were not shouting at the wind, it was the right thing to do.

End Note

The Second Moratorium to End the War in Vietnam on 15 November 1969 was the largest protest in American history to that date. While it failed to bring about the immediate end to the war sought by protesters, it did constitute a watershed of sorts in US foreign policy.

Richard Nixon campaigned for the presidency in 1968 on vague promises of an 'honorable end to the war in Vietnam'. The anti-war movement resolved to force Nixon's hand through inexorable public pressure. The protests continued, reaching a new low when four students were shot dead and nine more were wounded by panicked national guardsmen on the campus of Kent State University in May 1970. To put it in Machiavellian terms, it seemed that the greater the public strife, the more positive it was for the anti-war movement.

In Washington DC, any talk of victory was a distant memory. Now the corridors of power were abuzz with the strategy of 'Vietnamisation'—the empowering of the South Vietnamese forces to fight—and schedules for US troop withdrawals.

The American people grew tired of a costly war without end abroad, along with violent discord at home. A rising tide of public sentiment simply wanted to wash America's hands of the whole sorry business.

Initial overtures to end the war took place in May 1968, when President Lyndon Johnson sent American diplomats to Paris to meet with a delegation from North Vietnam. However, negotiations quickly foundered in the face of hardball tactics by the North Vietnamese, who saw the discord on the home front as a sign of American weakness.

In August 1969, Nixon dispatched his National Security Adviser, Henry Kissinger, to a secret meeting in France with North Vietnamese politburo member Lê Đức Thọ. Negotiations then dragged on for three years, while Nixon presided over a reduction of American troops from 475,000 in 1969 to 24,000 in 1972. A diplomatic breakthrough was finally achieved when the US abandoned its pledge to support the regime of South Vietnamese President Nguyễn Văn Thiệu. Only when Nixon essentially agreed to unconditional withdrawal, were the North Vietnamese willing to sign a peace deal.

A detailed account of the twists and turns of diplomacy that ended the Vietnam War is beyond the scope of this story. I am merely trying to provide the reader with a brief overview of events that were set in train by the anti-war movement in which I played a very minor role.

I suppose it might be fair to say that the Vietnam War was a misapplication of the diplomatic lessons of the 1930s, but Hanoi was not Munich, and permitting the Vietnamese people to secure their own destiny was not appeasement of a megalomaniacal dictator.

Yet while the death and destruction wrought by the war was horrific, for the sake of accuracy it must be noted that the human toll during the post-war period was no less disastrous. Close to a million so-called boat people fled communist rule in Vietnam, with between 200,000 and 400,000 dying at sea from pirates or inclement weather. Another two million innocents were killed in Cambodia under the perverted Maoist rule of the Khmer Rouge.

Furious debate still rages among historians over the moral responsibility for the catastrophes that engulfed South-East Asia after the US withdrawal from Vietnam in 1975. I can assure you that an end to US involvement in Vietnam was unavoidable, inevitable and righteous. After two inconclusive wars of containment—Korea and Vietnam—and facing economic problems at home, by the early 1970s the American people no longer had the stomach for the fight.

'Moratorium March' to end the war in Vietnam, Washington, 15 November 1969

12. DEATH OF A REVOLUTIONARY: GEORGE JACKSON AND THE SOLEDAD BROTHERS

21 August 1971

> Black men born in the US and fortunate enough to live past the age of eighteen are conditioned to accept the inevitability of prison. For most of us, it simply looms as the next phase in a sequence of humiliations.

So wrote George Jackson, who entered Soledad State Prison himself on 12 January 1960.

Memories of that first day in adult prison never left George. In his prison letters, he wrote that being captured and imprisoned was 'the closest to being dead that one is likely to experience in this life.' In prison he was reduced to a number—inmate A63837.

Jackson's father was a postal worker and his overprotective mother rarely allowed George to leave the house. Initially, they lived in one of the oldest parts of Chicago, a mixture of ghetto, residential suburb and industrial area. A railroad track ran past the front of the Jackson apartment; there were factories over the road and garages and shops beneath. Soon they moved to a small, three-room apartment built over a tavern. Here their outdoor area was over the place where people deposited their garbage.

In a letter to an editor who'd requested his autobiography, Jackson wrote that he didn't see a white person until he started kindergarten. Growing up in a segregated neighbourhood, he'd approached the first white boy he'd seen and started feeling his hair and scratching his white skin. The boy hit Jackson in the head with a baseball bat and, he wrote: 'They found me crumpled in a heap just outside the schoolyard fence'.

After that experience, his mother sent him to St Malachy Catholic mission school. It was also in the ghetto. All the nuns were white and one of the priests was black. St Malachy's had two separate schools.

The private school was for white kids. It had a large garden with green grass and trees, picnic tables and playground equipment. There was a high, iron fence around it that served to keep the black kids out, Jackson remembered, and the white kids were driven to and from school in private buses or cars.

The second school, on the other side of the road, was for black kids. They played and fought on the corner sidewalks and back alleyways bordering the school and either walked or, when they could afford it, used the public buses or streetcars. For the first time, George's eyes were opened to the inequality and mistreatment of blacks in America and sparks of unrest were kindled within him.

The school ran from kindergarten to twelfth grade and Jackson attended for ten years, including kindergarten. During his school years, he spent most of the summers in southern Illinois with his grandmother and aunt, to remove him from harm's way, according to his mother. He learned how to shoot rifles, shotguns and pistols, and could leave the house without having to sneak out the window. He shot a lot of small animals, such as birds, rabbits and squirrels, and later admitted he felt guilty about it.

He spoke warmly of his grandfather, calling him George 'Papa' Davis. Papa lived and worked in Chicago, and 'was an extremely aggressive man', Jackson recalled. 'He was in jail now and then. I loved him. He died … in the fifth year that I was in San Quentin, on a pension that, after rent, allowed for a diet of little more than sardines and crackers.'

When the family moved into the Troop Street housing projects, Jackson's run-ins with the law really began. He and his siblings were often hungry. 'Our activities went from stolen food to other things I wanted,' he wrote. 'Gloves for my hands (which were always cold) and marbles for slingshots.' As a teenager he became increasingly restless and rebellious and was detained once or twice for mugging.

All his life, Jackson had pretended to his parents. 'I served mass so that I could be in a position to steal altar wine, sang in the choir because they made me,' he wrote later. He lived two lives: one with his family, the other on the street. He moved up and down the state and did what he wanted. When it came time to explain, he lied. Most of his time and money went on girls he met on the stairwells of the projects' fifteen-storey buildings.

But as Jackson grew older, his transgressions became impossible to hide. Mortified by his son's behaviour in Chicago, Jackson's father transferred his post-office job to Los Angeles in 1956, when George was fifteen. Alas, his son's problems with the law continued despite the family's change of locale.

Police began to pick him up on suspicion of crimes, or because he was in the wrong part of town. Jackson wrote, 'Except for once or twice I was never actually caught breaking any laws.' There was no possibility of a policeman catching him, either, he boasted. 'Through a gangway with a gate that only few can operate with speed (it's dark even in the day), up a stairway through a door. Across roofs with seven- to ten-foot jumps in between ...', there wasn't a cop 'in the city' who could keep up with him.

Jackson wrote of his father's shame at having to bail him out after encounters with the law, but he was never abandoned by his father.

Jackson was incarcerated in the California Youth Authority Corrections Facility in Paso Robles for breaking into a large department store in downtown Los Angeles. A police officer shot him six times at point-blank range as he stood with his hands in the air. After the second shot, when Jackson was certain that the officer was trying to murder him, Jackson charged him. Later, when Jackson was recalling this event, he wrote, 'Since all blacks are thought of as rats, the third degree started before I was taken to hospital. Medical treatment was offered as a reward for cooperation.'

A month before the department store arrest, Jackson had bought a motorcycle and the documentation provided by the owner turned out to be a forgery. The bike was hot and he was caught riding it. There was nothing he could do, and the two events, when considered together, meant Jackson was sent to Paso Robles.

'It was like dying,' Jackson later wrote. 'Just to exist at all in the cage calls for some heavy psychic readjustments. It is the thing I have been running from all my life.'

When prison first caught up with him in 1957, Jackson was fifteen years old. The staff at Paso Robles were 'the same general types found lounging at all prison facilities,' wrote Jackson. 'They need a job—any job; the state needs goons … one must cease to resist altogether or else.'

From day to day, Jackson merely existed to avoid lockup. Food and rest were strictly controlled and nobody could move from their bed after lights out. There were so many regulations that, despite their best efforts, very few inmates managed to stay out of trouble. Every part of daily life was programmed down to the smallest detail. They were even made to march in military fashion to the gym, the mess hall, to compulsory prayer meetings and everywhere else it seemed.

The strict regimentation of life within Paso Robles wore Jackson down. 'All my life I've done exactly what I wanted to do just when I wanted,' he wrote. 'No more, perhaps less sometimes, but never anymore.' When these words were written many years later, Jackson estimated he'd spent half his life in prison and still hadn't adjusted to it. 'I cannot truthfully say prison is any less painful now than during that first experience,' he noted.

After his release, Jackson stopped in Bakersfield, where he planned to stay a week or two. As it happened, he met a woman he liked and ended up staying longer. Jackson wrote that he and a couple of other youths borrowed a car and 'went off'. They robbed a petrol station of $71 at gunpoint. Jackson was eighteen and already burdened with an arrest record for various thefts, muggings and other petty offences. Jackson was advised by his court-appointed attorney to plead guilty. He agreed to cut a plea deal, that would spare the state the expense of a trial, in return for a lighter prison sentence. Jackson later told a friend, 'The record that the state has compiled on my activities reads like the record of ten men. It labels me brigand, thief, burglar, gambler, hobo, drug addict, gunman … escape artist.' Jackson was promised a sentence of one year or less.

Instead, the judge imposed a sentence of 'one year to life', a term of imprisonment where the prisoner's release is at the discretion of the California Parole Board.

Once in prison, Jackson realised guards at Soledad and San Quentin conspired to provoke black prisoners with racial slurs and fostered violence among inmates. In some instances, prison staff even passed weapons to their favoured inmates.

As Jackson told it, prison staff encouraged white prisoners to throw excrement into the cells of black inmates and mix urine, glass and cleaning powder into their food. He chose to resist this systemic mistreatment, and as a result, his parole applications were repeatedly denied. Prison became his world. As he later wrote, 'The feeling of being captured ... this slave can never adjust to it; it's a thing that I just don't favor, then, now, never.'

His only respite from the rigours of imprisonment was when he could sit down and write 'convict letters' to his family and friends on the single sheet of ruled paper he was permitted.

During his time in jail, Jackson read the works of Marx, Lenin, Trotsky, Engels and Mao. These radicalised and, in his eyes, redeemed him. He also met other incarcerated black nationalists including George 'Big Jake' Lewis, James Carr, W L Nolen, Bill Christmas, Torry Gibson and many others. An entire new political philosophy opened before him—one that he would never be able to pursue beyond prison walls.

Jackson was drawn into political activism, seeking to preserve his human rights, assert his black identity and attract attention to the appalling conditions in Soledad and San Quentin. He joined the Black Panthers and became an organiser, seeing himself as a revolutionary fighting against an unjust society rather than as an offender.

In a letter to his father in 1965, Jackson wrote, 'Pure nonviolence as a political ideal, then, is absurd. Politics is violence … If this agitation that we like to term as nonviolent is to have any meaning at all we must force the fascist to taste the bitterness of our wrath.'

As a result of this activism, Jackson, and many others, were subjected to years of vicious retribution by the state. He spent more than eleven years in prison, in and out of isolation for alleged assaults, often as a response to 'race talk' or threats of lynching by the guards.

Jackson remembered in his early prison years reading *The Lion's Skin* by Rafael Sabatini, a story of the hunted stalking the hunter—the most predatory animal on Earth turning on its oppressor and killing him. It was an epiphany. 'I dreamed of smashing my enemies entirely, overwhelming, vanquishing, crushing them completely, sinking my fangs into the hunter's neck and never, never letting go,' he wrote in one of the many letters published in *Soledad Brother*.

Jackson's politics were also informed by external events, but they crystalised during his incarceration. The sixties in the United States was a decade of political and racial turbulence, a period marked by civil rights sit-ins, freedom rides and assassinations—Malcolm X, Martin Luther King, Jr, President John F Kennedy and his brother, Robert Kennedy. Race riots, Vietnam War demonstrations and protests at the Chicago Convention of the Democratic Party were met with violent police repression, and police raided the Black Panthers. Republican Richard Nixon was elected president on a 'law and order' political platform.

Towards the end of the 1960s, racial tensions were high at Soledad and prisoners were segregated into racial groups. On 13 January 1970, a new exercise yard opened. White guards taunted black prisoners and when the yard opened ten white and seven black prisoners were selected to enter. Some of the blacks were well-known political activists, while many of the whites were known to be racist. A guard with a semi-automatic rifle was stationed in a small tower at the corner of the yard. Unsurprisingly, a fight broke out between the groups of prisoners. In response, the tower guard opened fire, killing three black prisoners and wounding one white prisoner. Within three days, a grand jury announced that the shootings were 'justifiable homicide'.

Most of the black prisoners, and many white prisoners in Soledad, went on a hunger strike in protest over the grand jury's refusal to indict. Half an hour later, a white guard by the name of John Mills was found fatally injured in Jackson's wing after being beaten and thrown from an upper floor of the cell block.

A few days later, Jackson, John Clutchette and Fleeta Drumgo were charged with the murder, becoming known as the 'Soledad Brothers'. Because Jackson's original conviction of second-degree robbery was technically a life sentence, this new charge carried a mandatory death penalty.

When asked during a media interview whether he'd been involved in the killing of Mills, Jackson smiled and replied cryptically, 'Look, one of the most important elements of guerrilla warfare is maintaining secrecy. I've killed nobody until it's been proven. And they'll never be able to prove anything like that.'

Jackson was cynical about what he regarded as a racially biased justice system. In a letter to his attorney, Fay Stender, he described how three unarmed black prisoners had been shot dead by a white guard who was completely exonerated, but when one white guard was subsequently killed, three black prisoners faced the gas chamber.

The prosecution of the three Soledad Brothers opened with two secret hearings in the Salinas County Courthouse, which had jurisdiction over the prison. A third hearing was about to take place when Soledad Brother John Clutchette smuggled a note to his mother that read, 'Help, I'm in trouble.'

Clutchette's mother enlisted the help of several politicians who, in turn, enlisted a legal defence team to assist the accused men. The Soledad Brothers' attorneys initially met with resistance from the prosecuting authorities. Defence lawyers were denied access to witnesses and, when permission was finally obtained, they found that the witnesses had been intimidated and were frightened.

The defence attorneys were also denied access to the scene of the crime. By the time they were able to visit the interior of Soledad Prison, they found that an additional staircase had been built, making it difficult to evaluate the testimony of eyewitnesses.

Then there was the issue of prison records. In a blatant violation of the Supreme Court's so-called 'Brady Rule', the defence team was denied access to prison logs, while at the same time the prosecution was able to study them at will. Yet defence attorneys managed to obtain a change of venue for the trial to San Francisco, away from the Soledad area where the press had already pronounced the men guilty and deserving of the death penalty.

Jackson gave vent to his fears in his letters to Fay Stender. He'd been the victim of so many racist attacks, he explained, he'd never be able to relax again. They'd never count him among the broken men, but after ten years in prison—including seven in solitary—he'd never be normal either. 'I just lit my seventy-seventh cigarette of this twenty-one-hour day ...' he wrote. 'I can still smile sometimes, but by the time this thing is over I may not be a nice person.'

Within weeks, the Soledad Brothers' case emerged as a *cause célèbre* for those demanding social change. There was already a mass movement against the Vietnam War, and now American institutions in more than a hundred cities were shaken by rioting. Support for Jackson and his fellow defendants grew, and defence committees were formed to raise funds in San Francisco and Los Angeles. Activist Angela Davis, a self-professed Black Panther and member of the American Communist Party, who was fighting her own dismissal from the University of California on ideological grounds, became a prominent supporter of the Los Angeles Defense Committee.

At the end of 1969, Jackson's younger brother Jonathan was a sixteen-year-old high-school student in Pasadena. He worshipped his older brother and each day as he sat in the schoolyard gulping his Coke and eating his salami sandwich, he became more upset by the injustice of his brother's long imprisonment and the murder charges against him.

In January 1970, George Jackson was transferred to San Quentin. Six months later, on 18 June 1970, in an underground paper at his school, Jonathan wrote, 'People have said I am obsessed with my brother's case ... it's true. I don't laugh very much anymore. I have but one question to ask all of you and the people that think like you: What would you do if it was your brother?'

Then, on 7 August that same year, Jonathan walked into the San Rafael Courthouse where another San Quentin prisoner was on trial. He sat in the courtroom for a few short moments, then quickly rose from the audience and pulled a folding-stock carbine from under his jacket, snarling, 'All right everybody, this is it!'

Judge Harold Haley watched in horror as Jonathan reached down and snatched two additional pistols and a sawn-off shotgun from his satchel. In the chaos that followed, Jonathan threw his extra guns to the prisoner and the witnesses in the holding bay. He and the other kidnappers took Judge Haley, the male deputy district attorney, and three female jurors, hostage.

As they scrambled out of the courtroom, Jonathan shouted, 'We are the revolutionaries! Free the Soledad Brothers by 12.30.' The kidnappers marched their hostages out of the court and into an elevator. Once in the lobby, they forced them outside into a waiting van.

As the van started to move away from the courthouse there was a barrage of fire from police who had set up nearby. In the shootout that followed, Judge Haley, Jonathan Jackson and two other prisoners were shot dead.

By all accounts, Jackson approved of his younger brother's evolution from an innocent child of ten into a militant revolutionary of seventeen, but Jonathan's death still jolted him. Reflecting on his brother's fate, a despondent Jackson wrote, 'He was free for a while. I guess that's more than most of us can expect.'

A few days after the attack, it was discovered that the guns used by Jonathan Jackson had been registered in the name of Angela Davis. A warrant was immediately issued for Davis's arrest. Shortly thereafter, she appeared on the FBI's Ten Most Wanted list. Her picture appeared under the heading, 'Wanted for murder and kidnapping', along with the description, 'considered highly dangerous'. These words were generally accepted to mean that the fugitive could be killed at the slightest hint of resistance during arrest. Nonetheless, Davis was apprehended without incident some weeks later in New York.

By now, the case of the Soledad Brothers had become controversial and was heavy with racial overtones. The defendants and their supporters maintained that the prosecution was an act of political repression by the government. In San Francisco, preparations for the trial were underway. A bulletproof glass and steel barrier was erected to separate spectators from the well of the court. Attorneys for the three Soledad Brothers argued unsuccessfully for the removal of the barrier. They also moved successfully for the recusal of Presiding Judge Walter J Carpeneti on the grounds that he was racially prejudiced. The trial was postponed for two weeks until a new judge could be found.

On 21 August 1971, the now twenty-nine-year-old Jackson waited in San Quentin State Prison to see his attorney. It was a warm summer's day, the sky cloudy, the breeze light. George Jackson was no longer young and energetic; prison had aged him beyond his years. His black hair was already greying, his face was pallid and his skin marred by spots.

At 1.15 pm Jackson put his blue prison denims back on after a body search and followed a guard from the Adjustment Center, where the most difficult inmates were held, across the courtyard to the Prison Visitor Center.

At 1.25 pm Stephen Bingham, Jackson's attorney, passed through the electronic gate and walked across the corner of the main visiting room where, on either side of long tables, families were sitting across from inmates talking. The guard on duty opened the door to the 'A' visiting room and let Bingham inside. Another guard brought Jackson in through the steel door that opened off a tunnel from the prison interior. The two men—attorney and prisoner-client—were then locked inside a two-by-three-metre chamber with white walls and a single, barred window.

They conferred until about 2.25 pm except for a short time when Bingham left to smoke a cigarette. During the attorney's absence, Jackson sat still, his forehead in the palms of his hands, his elbows on the table. He had no choice but to sit and wait. The air inside the meeting room was thick and heavy. His mindset was reflected in a quote later published by the San Francisco *Good Times*, an alternative Bay Area newspaper, 'I'll never forgive, I'll never forget, and if I'm guilty of anything at all it's of not leaning on them hard enough.' This was a desperate inner scream—a plea from his soul, begging to be heard.

Now, sitting in the small room in San Quentin Prison waiting for his attorney, Bingham, to return, Jackson may well have been thinking of the words he once wrote to his mother, 'Should I fail, you are not to say, "George is no good". You must try to understand that now, just as in the past, there are other considerations and influences that enter into the course of events that turn our lives one way or the other.'

When his attorney returned to the visiting room, Jackson looked up and spoke in a hushed voice. At about 2.25 pm Bingham turned and waved to the guard. The guard entered and then Bingham rose and announced, 'My visit is over.' Bingham nodded to Jackson as he left the room. The guard then led Jackson back across the courtyard and, at 2.27 pm, signed the register to record that Jackson had been returned to the Adjustment Center. Before entering his cell, Jackson stood on the walkway between Sergeant Kenneth McCray and Officer Rubiaco, waiting to be searched.

According to prison reports, Rubiaco noticed something like a pencil protruding from Jackson's hair. Rubiaco reached for it, but Jackson stepped back, ripped off his wig and grabbed a pistol and ammunition hidden beneath it. He scrambled to load the pistol and screamed, 'This is it!' He ordered the guard to open the cell and free the other prisoners.

A group of prisoners grabbed McCray, threw a cloth over his head, bound his hands and dragged him into Jackson's cell. There they slashed his throat with a shiv made from a razorblade and toothbrush. Then they slashed Rubiaco's throat and tossed him on top of McCray. A third guard's throat was cut, then he was strangled with an electric cord and shot in the back of the head, his body thrown onto the pile. A fourth officer was strangled and his throat slashed. Another officer suffered the same fate and was left for dead, while two white inmates had their throats cut. In all, five people were murdered; McCray and Rubiaco survived the attack.

The prison warden stated that Jackson was spotted with a gun and the alarm was sounded at 2.40 pm. Inside the Adjustment Center, Sergeant Graham encountered Jackson who forced him into his cell. The sergeant was then shot in the back of the head and killed, execution style. The bullet lodged at the base of the sergeant's skull and was later recovered. It was compared by microscope with other bullets test-fired from the gun that was in Jackson's possession when the officer was killed. Officials refused to declare the result of the forensic comparison because they said they wanted to 'save it for the trial'.

The official account of events states that shortly after the alarm went off, Jackson pushed open the Adjustment Center's outer door and ran across the yard to a passage winding downhill alongside the north wall of the prison. According to the prison warden, a guard on the wall south of the Adjustment Center then shot and killed George Jackson.

Jackson's autopsy revealed that he'd been hit by two bullets. The fatal shot entered the top of his head and shattered his skull, continued down the front of his spine, breaking two ribs, and exited through his lower back. By the warden's official account, that bullet hit Jackson's body from behind. Yet forensic analysis says that this same bullet entered his body from the front and exited through his back. This discrepancy between the official account of the shooting and the autopsy report has never been reconciled by the California Department of Corrections.

In 1971, *The New York Times* put together a reconstruction of the afternoon at San Quentin that led to Jackson's death. It surmised that a first shot from the guard on the south wall may have hit Jackson's ankle and knocked him down. Jackson then struggled to his feet, facing south, when the fatal shot struck him in the head.

Georgia Jackson, George's mother, said she believed her son was murdered inside the Adjustment Center and his body dragged outside by guards. The pistol that Jackson was alleged to be carrying was twenty centimetres long, thirteen centimetres high and three centimetres thick. It is implausible that he would be able to conceal a weapon of that size under a wig.

After Jackson's death, attorneys for the surviving Soledad Brothers met with their clients and held a press conference in San Francisco. The attorneys were caustic about the version of events provided by the prison authorities. As one attorney said, 'From everything we've been able to gather, there was no escape attempt—certainly not with respect to any of the men that we represent.'

The same attorney revealed that their clients reported the sounds of a scuffle and then gunfire. Ordered to come out of their cells and stand against the wall, they heard machine-gun fire, the lawyer said, before they were ordered to strip naked, after which they were handcuffed and made to walk outside and lie face down on the lawn.

The warden said it took twenty-five minutes for reinforcements to regain control. 'A machine-gun burst of four or five shots was fired into the Adjustment Center,' he said, and a prisoner had shouted, 'We've got hostages.'

A guard responded, 'That won't do you any good.' Then one by one, the prisoners emerged as the guards went into the Center to find McCray and Rubiaco injured, but alive, and five dead.

Jackson had died before his trial for the murder of prison guard John Mills could begin. His supporters believe he was murdered by prison authorities because the Black Panther Party, of which he was a prominent member, posed a serious threat to their authority.

Black American author James Baldwin said he didn't believe a weapon had been smuggled into San Quentin Prison and he called for an investigation, saying, 'No black person will ever believe that George Jackson died the way they tell us he did.'

END NOTE

When the prison shooting death of American black revolutionary George Jackson was reported in Australian newspapers in 1971, I was a university student. For pragmatic reasons, I had chosen to study accounting, but although I was good with numbers, I found them uninspiring. Instead, I would hang out with history, politics and philosophy students who were constantly debating moral and cultural questions, great and small. I found it fascinating.

It was those humanities students who first drew my attention to the story of George Jackson. The more I learned about the circumstances of his life and his death, the more profound became the sense of injustice I felt. Since that time, I've worked, in whatever modest way I can, to promote the cause of racial reconciliation here in Australia, but much remains to be done.

Perhaps Rabbi Hillel said it best, 'It is not incumbent upon you to complete this work; but neither are you at liberty to desist from it.'

13. THE EQUAL RIGHTS AMENDMENT AND WOMEN'S STRIKE FOR EQUALITY

1923–82, 1971

'Annie, get in here!' The commanding voice echoed through the office.

'Coming.'

I hurried into the next room where Bella Abzug stood, a stout, middle-aged woman in a polka-dot dress, holding a wide-brimmed hat in each hand.

'Which one?' she asked.

I paused before answering. 'The plain red straw. Goes well with your dress and it'll look good on TV.'

'Red it is,' said Abzug as she tossed the hat atop the jumbled mass of papers on her desk.

'We need to go. It'll take us at least forty minutes to get to the Village. We don't want to be late for the broadcast.'

'Honey,' grinned Abzug, 'I'm the star attraction. Arriving fashionably late will only increase my appeal.' Nevertheless, she scooped up her hat, jammed it on her head and marched out the door.

We came out of our office building onto the sidewalk of Central Park West, where I hailed a passing taxi.

'NYU,' I instructed the driver. 'Waverly Place and Washington Square East, please, and hurry.'

'You got it,' the driver said in a broad Brooklyn accent as he edged the taxi into southbound traffic.

I felt Abzug's look of appraisal as the taxi swung around Columbus Circle into W 57th Street and lowered my gaze to the leather portfolio on my lap. It was a gift from my parents on my graduation from Radcliffe.

'Out with it,' she barked as we turned south on Fifth Avenue, the site of that extraordinary march back in 1970. 'What's bugging you?'

I sighed. Opening my portfolio, I extracted a sheet of paper adorned with the Veritas Shield of Harvard University.

Abzug snatched the letter from my grasp. 'So, you got in,' she said. 'You're abandoning me.'

I returned her smile. 'Largely because of your letter of recommendation.'

'Total bullshit,' declared Abzug with the caustic bluntness for which she was famous ... or, in some quarters, notorious. 'Don't sell yourself short. And don't forget about me once you become one of those fancy Harvard lawyers.'

'I'll remember,' I replied.

I'd remember much more than that, I thought. Bella had been my heroine from the early anti-war days when she'd established Women Strike for Peace with Dagmar Wilson. In 1961, around fifty thousand women marched in cities across the US to demonstrate for peace and against nuclear weapons. Then nine years later, on 26 August 1970, I was there marching with other women in the Women's Strike for Equality, calling for free abortion, equal opportunity in the workforce and free childcare. The strike also called for political rights for women, and social equality and equal rights for women in marriage. At the time of the protest women earned fifty-nine cents for every dollar a man earned for similar work, women were restricted from higher education, and in many states, women were not even allowed to obtain credit cards, make a will, or own property without a husband's permission. Can you imagine twenty thousand or so women gathering on Fifth Avenue carrying signs with, 'Don't Iron while the Strike is Hot', 'Hardhats for Soft Broads' and 'We are the 51% Minority'. So effective was Mrs Abzug in her advocacy that she convinced President Nixon to issue a proclamation anointing that date—26 August—as Women's Equality Day, introducing the bill herself. There was much to remember about Bella Abzug and much to be grateful for.

'Thank you, Bella,' I said, turning to smile at her.

'Well-earned and well-deserved,' she replied in a clipped tone. 'Got my notes?'

'Right here.'

I pulled a manila folder from my portfolio and handed it to my boss. The rest of the cab ride passed in silence as she studied her notes.

Finally, the taxi lurched to a halt in front of the Main Building, which housed New York University's College of Arts and Sciences. I paid the driver and we entered the building, following the buzz of conversation that was coming from Hemmerdinger Hall.

On entering, we saw an auditorium filled with nearly two hundred people seated before an elevated stage. An NYU banner was hanging behind a coffee table in the middle of a semicircle of three chairs. A speakers podium, portable floodlights and three TV cameras on wheeled mounts completed preparations for the upcoming show.

A tall, silver-haired man clad in a tailored suit and bow tie made his way towards us with extended hand. I recognised him as William F Buckley, founder and editor of *National Review* magazine, an icon of American conservatism.

'Welcome, Mrs Abzug,' said Buckley, in his mellifluous, patrician accent.

'Thank you, Mr Buckley,' Abzug replied as she took the proffered hand. 'This is my assistant, Anne Kauffman, who'll be leaving me soon to study law at Harvard.'

'Well, as a Yale man I'll try not to hold that against you,' quipped Buckley as he graced me with a smile that reeked of *noblesse oblige*.

I responded with a hasty smile of my own as I settled into a front-row seat.

'Mrs Schlafly has yet to arrive,' said Buckley, while accompanying Abzug onto the stage where a team of TV studio staff descended on her to connect her microphone and touch up her make-up.

Buckley and my boss had just settled into their seats—she stage left and he in the middle—when a tall, fiftyish woman with neatly coiffed blonde hair entered the auditorium.

A chorus of boos erupted until Buckley rose from his seat and strode to the edge of the stage. 'Ladies and gentlemen, please!' he declared loudly, cutting through the audience's heckling. 'Here, we pride ourselves on a civil exchange of ideas. Please honour that principle. Thank you.'

'Hello, Phyllis,' Buckley greeted the new arrival with a friendly familiarity that bespoke long acquaintance.

Schlafly ascended the stage and deposited a chaste kiss on Buckley's cheek before exchanging a brief handshake with Abzug. Then she promptly settled into the chair on stage right.

'Three minutes,' yelled a man wearing a headset and mic combination—the producer, apparently.

The three cameramen assumed their places behind the TV cameras, putting on similar headsets, flipping switches and turning dials.

The producer turned to address the audience. 'Ladies and gentlemen, we will be going live in a few minutes. Please respect the privilege of being part of our live audience and remain silent throughout the program.'

'Thirty seconds to live,' the producer announced a couple of minutes later.

'Ten, nine, eight, seven, six, five, four,' he counted down, signalling the final three digits to zero with his fingers before making a tomahawk gesture with his right hand.

'Funding for Firing Line is provided by stations of the Public Broadcasting System,' blared a pre-recorded message through a loudspeaker, 'Dow Chemical Company, the Mobil Corporation, John M Olin Foundation Incorporated, Laurel Foundation, Atlantic Richfield and the Friends of Firing Line.'

The opening strains of Bach's Brandenburg Concerto No. 2 echoed from the speaker as one of the cameras panned through the audience before zooming in for a close-up on Buckley.

'The proposal for a constitutional amendment to provide for equality of the sexes was the topic of intense debate even before its introduction to Congress last October. As of today, November 12th, 1972, the Rights Amendment, or ERA, has been passed by both houses of Congress and ratified by twenty-two state legislatures. That is sixteen states shy of thirty-eight, the magic number required to amend our constitution.'

Buckley paused as he shuffled his notes.

'With us tonight to discuss this contentious issue are the most prominent proponents for each side. Arguing in favour of the ERA is Congresswoman Bella Abzug who represents the Upper West Side of Manhattan. She's an alumna of Columbia University Law School and has become one of the most prominent public voices advocating for the Equal Rights Amendment. Two years ago, she played a major role in the Women's Strike for Equality, a nationwide protest of more than fifty thousand women, spearheaded by Betty Friedan. Ladies and gentlemen, please welcome Congresswoman Abzug.'

Buckley looked up from his notes and smiled, triggering enthusiastic applause from the audience.

Abzug beamed as Buckley continued. 'Arguing in opposition is Mrs Phyllis Schlafly, founder of STOP ERA, a movement of conservative women whose purpose is self-evident from its title. Mrs Schlafly is a graduate of Washington University in St Louis and Radcliffe College. She is married and is the mother of six children. I ask that you welcome her with the same courtesy you showed to her opponent.'

The applause was tepid by comparison to the welcome for Abzug, but this was New York City, after all.

'We'll begin proceedings with each of our debaters presenting their case in a five-minute argument. This will be followed by a one-minute rebuttal each, before we transition into a more informal discussion for the remainder of the hour. Mrs Abzug, the floor is yours.'

'Thank you, Mr Buckley.' Abzug rose from her seat and walked to the podium.

'Ladies and gentlemen, a piece of unfinished business sits at the heart of our republic. Unfinished business means we've yet to fulfil the transcendent ideals expressed in those glorious founding documents written almost two centuries ago. Thomas Jefferson wrote about the self-evident truth that all men were created equal. Yet he was a slave owner. The abomination of Jim Crow persisted until the passage of the Civil Rights Act, less than a decade ago. From the steps of the Lincoln Memorial, the late great Martin Luther King, Jr, spoke of our national default on the promissory note conveyed by our founding documents to our citizens who are black. Tonight, I humbly submit that America has likewise defaulted on the promise of equality made to that half of our population that is female.'

Abzug paused to pour herself a glass of water from which she took a sip.

'For well over a century after our nation's founding, the common law principle of coverture denied American married women the right to hold property or hold earnings separate and apart from their husbands. The Nineteenth Amendment granting women the right to vote was ratified in 1920, 130 years after the Constitution came into force. In both of those cases, and many others, this regime of sex-based discrimination against women was only abolished through legislative action, both statutory and constitutional.'

Abzug lifted her eyes from her notes and focused her gaze on the audience.

'Ladies and gentlemen, friends, I call on you to help forge the great missing link in the struggle for American civil rights, the Equal Rights Amendment. It will demolish the last vestiges of legalised second-class citizenship that apply to every second person in our nation. So here is what I ask. Let us go forth arm in arm—blacks and whites, women and men, young people and the elderly—to make good on that most foundational of American principles—equality. Thank you very much.'

A crescendo of applause swept through the room as Abzug resumed her seat.

'Mrs Schlafly, the floor is yours.'

Phyllis Schlafly took to the podium and graced the audience with a broad, self-confident smile. 'Thank you, Bill, and I thank my husband for allowing me to speak here tonight.'

The rumble of burgeoning outrage erupted from the audience until Buckley rose to his feet.

'Ladies and gentlemen, please! The ethos of *Firing Line* is the civil exchange of divergent views, no matter how offensive some might find them. For my part, I put aside my detestation of Marxism to host representatives of the Socialist Workers Party on this program. If I can listen with courtesy to the views of a Trotskyist, I would ask you to afford the same respect to Mrs Schlafly.'

'Thank you again, Bill,' said Schlafly, her head bowing in an appreciative nod.

'I realise full well that I do not enjoy the home-court advantage that my esteemed opponent can claim as her own. I am not a New Yorker, but rather a born-and-bred Midwesterner from the Show Me State of Missouri. I am not a left-of-centre agnostic, but a dyed-in-the-wool conservative Catholic who believes in traditional values of sex and family as conveyed by the Holy Bible. In other words, I must strike most of you in the audience as a curiosity at best and a dangerous zealot at worst. But if I may be so bold as to quote that arch-heretic Martin Luther, "Here I stand, I can do no other".'

13. The Equal Rights Amendment and Women's Strike for Equality

Schlafly examined her notes for a long moment.

'I do not mean to utilise this podium for a debate on the merits of the war in Vietnam. But it is a reality of our time that thousands of young American men are, as we speak, fighting in the jungles of South-East Asia. Over the past decade, over fifty thousand soldiers, sailors, marines and airmen have perished in the hellish fires of combat against a cruel enemy. And I ask, is this something we wish to inflict on the young women of our nation? Because, make no mistake ... the Equal Rights Amendment will impose military conscription on your daughters, sisters and perhaps even your wives.'

Schlafly paused for effect.

'Now, I am well aware that President Nixon ran on a platform of abolishing the draft and ending the war in Vietnam. So, doubtless, many of you in the audience believe that conscription is no longer a relevant issue. But as philosopher Immanuel Kant noted, "The state of peace among men living side by side is not the natural state; the natural state is one of war". That means someday, somewhere, American troops will once again be called on to take up arms against evil. So, the question you must ask yourselves is whether you're prepared to countenance female soldiers being captured and physically abused and flag-draped coffins filled with young women being interred at Arlington National Cemetery. This is something I am not prepared to accept. Not for my daughters. Not for my nieces. Not for any young American woman. And then there is the damage the ERA would do to the foundations of our society.'

A wave of derisive laughter swept over the audience, triggering a grim smile from Phyllis Schlafly.

'You may sneer, but it's my firm belief that passage of the ERA will undermine traditions of Western civilisation that have nurtured and protected traditional family structures for centuries. I'm a working woman myself, and fully support equality of opportunity for other women, but the ERA will place American society on a far more destructive path. One that leads to equality, not of opportunity, but of equal outcomes enforced by the coercive power of government. We'll see sex-based quotas that erode the principle of achievement on the basis of merit. We'll see homosexual marriage and the introduction of mixed-sex bathing and toilet facilities. Mark my words, ladies and gentlemen, the ERA will upend the foundations of American civilisation, and that I cannot abide. Thank you very much.'

There was no applause from the audience as Schlafly returned to her seat.

'Thank you very much to both our debaters for their articulate presentations,' said Buckley. 'Let me start with a question to Mrs Abzug. You argue that the same principles that applied to the civil rights movement for racial equality should now apply to women. But is race really equivalent to sex? While the differences between black men and white men are superficial, can the same be said for the difference between men and women?'

'Thank you for that question, Mr Buckley. For the purposes of this discussion, I would say that, yes, the two struggles are essentially the same. Just as there is no valid reason to deny black Americans entry to a school or university, there is no reason to deny women entry into the profession of their choice, and tradition be damned.'

'Yes, but picking up on a point raised by Mrs Schlafly, do you think that same principle should apply to the military? Should the army and marines have infantrywomen in their ranks?'

'Yes, Mr Buckley, they should, particularly in light of the fact that

13. The Equal Rights Amendment and Women's Strike for Equality

we're about to transition to an all-volunteer military. If a woman wants to fight for her country, why should we deny her that right?'

'But I would argue that military service is not a right,' smiled Buckley in response. 'The draft is called "Selective Service" for a reason. People with disabilities are denied enlistment all the time.'

Abzug gave a predatory grin. 'Mr Buckley, are you saying that being female is a disability?' she asked in a saccharine tone.

Raucous laughter and applause broke out in the audience as Buckley's cheeks reddened. 'No, not at all,' he protested. 'I am simply pointing out the fact that there are demonstrable physical differences between men and women that do not apply to people of different racial groups. Mrs Schlafly, you argued that the ERA would erode the structure of Western civilisation. Can you elaborate?'

'Thank you, Bill. Our society has evolved around traditional concepts of the nuclear family that have stood us in very good stead. Yes, of course, there is a minuscule minority of men who abuse their position to commit violence against their wives and children. Just as there are small criminal fringe elements that commit armed robbery and murder. But just as we do not tar the entire population with the crimes of that criminal fringe, so we should not blame all men for the abuse of that minuscule minority. For the overwhelming majority of people now and throughout the ages, traditional marriage has been a very good thing and we should not legislate unnecessary measures that will corrode it.'

'You still haven't explained how that will happen,' challenged Buckley.

Schlafly sighed, perhaps unaccustomed to serious questioning from people she considered political allies.

'All you have to do is read the writings of leading feminist thinkers. Germaine Greer calls for the overthrow of the traditional family structure in her book *The Female Eunuch*, and Betty Friedan does the same in *The Feminine Mystique*. These are radicals who seek to destroy ...'

Schlafly was interrupted mid-sentence by a thunderous blare that echoed through the room. I watched as Buckley rose to his feet, exchanging a look of alarm with his producer.

'Ladies and gentlemen, that is the fire alarm. Please make your way in a calm and orderly fashion out of the building. Thank you.'

I joined Abzug as she descended from the stage and we made our way through an exit. After several twists and turns through a corridor we found ourselves on the sidewalk of Greene Street behind Main Hall.

'If I knew who pulled that alarm, I'd kiss them,' growled Abzug. 'There's only so much shit I can take at one sitting.'

'Yeah,' I agreed, 'she was laying it on thick.'

We shared a laugh and I decided to take advantage of my boss's good mood.

'Are we done for tonight?' I asked.

'Sure,' she grinned. 'See you tomorrow bright and early. We have to keep up the fight.'

'Good night, Bella.'

'Good night, dear.'

I remained with Bella Abzug's congressional office for another ten months before decamping to Harvard Law. While my primary focus over the following three years was my legal studies, I followed the ratification progress of the Equal Rights Amendment through the legislatures of the states. I revelled with each new ratification and was outraged when Nebraska and Tennessee passed resolutions repealing their previous approvals of the ERA.

After graduation from law school in May of 1976, I began

to work as a federal public defender at the Southern District of New York in Manhattan, but I also found time to moonlight as speechwriter for Abzug's unsuccessful campaigns for the US Senate and mayor of New York City.

As the seven-year ratification deadline approached in 1979, it was clear that the ERA would fall short of the ten states required for constitutional adoption. So, 22 March found me at a wine bar in Greenwich Village drowning my feminist sorrows with Bella Abzug in a bottle of Chateau Pontet-Canet and nibbling at bar snacks.

'So, what's next for you, Bella? Are you going to run again for office?'

'Don't know,' she shrugged. 'Losing to Moynihan in the Senate primary was bad enough, but coming in fourth in the Democratic race for New York mayor really stung. I don't know if I have it in me to run again.'

'Come on now,' I said. 'Voted the third most influential House member and one of the twenty most influential women in the world?'

'Yeah, yeah, but there's a whole world out there. Perhaps I should look further afield.'

'The UN?' I asked.

'Maybe.' She fell silent, staring into her wine, and for a moment I thought I saw a flicker of something like uncertainty.

'Do you remember that debate with Phyllis Schlafly?' I asked.

'Do I ever,' Abzug laughed. 'I was about to rip her argument to shreds and that damned fire alarm went off.'

'Saved by the bell?' I asked with eyebrow arched.

'You better believe it,' she declared with a grin. Bella Abzug, armed and dangerous once more. Yes, the ERA had failed to pass, but life was good nonetheless, and we both lived to fight another day.